HELSINKI

Helsingfors

Hel

sinki »

THE CITY OF HELSINKI

Prologue

This book is not a portrait of Helsinki. It is not even a single writer's interpretation of the city, one story in one time, framed within one frame. We did not wish for a book like that.

Naturally, we each interpret Helsinki according to our experiences and opinions. Frequent visitors notice that these interpretations vary as times and views change. Not one person has only one story of this city and so we wished to show Helsinki as it appears from time to time - actually all the time.

This book is a collection of how different people under different circumstances, at different times and in different frames of mind, encounter Helsinki's people, buildings, stories, services, historic monuments, nature and much more. This we wished to do because, actually, that's how it is: now, soon and sometimes was. The city lives at different times and looks, smells and feels different all the time, even though not one of us notices it at one and the same time.

There were dozens of pictorial observers: Photographic students from the University of Art and Design went everywhere, following their own impulses or in the tracks of others, searching for something new, different, dissimilar, that did not as yet exist. The literary observers were fewer in number but they covered an immense field: Anna-Stina Nykänen is a journalist who has recently started writing about sport, Antti Raivio is a playwright, director and founder of a theatre, Jonni Roos is a cultural journalist, Pirkko Saisio is a professor and writer, and Märta Tikkanen and Kjell Westö are both writers. Harri Ruohomäki, who has written up the Helsinki vignettes, is a communications consultant and media producer.

> Harri Ruohomäki

14

30

58

60

64

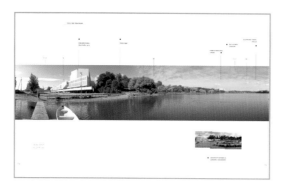

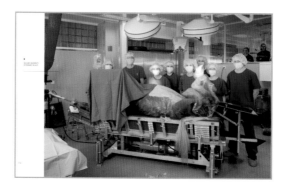

A dreamy dream

Here's that guy again. Time after time, even if others come more often. But this one's so odd: he comes up to the bar, sits down, has a beer, sometimes a whisky, and never says a word. Hours on end. Well, he talks in a way like, to himself – no sound emerges, but his expression changes, like he's listening to something new. Or perhaps he's just pretending.

I mean, I've nothing against that, others shout like urban apes after they've had a couple. Now he's on a pint of Three Lager and I bet you a hundred marks he won't say a word.

"Thanks, keep the change. You know, I've been having this odd dream. D'you mind if I tell you about it?"

Now what's happening. He talks. And we've been looking at each other over the bar for at least three years.

"Yea. Why not. Fire away."

"Well, it always starts like this: it's late afternoon, in spring. I'm in my flat, where I can see the living room and the kitchen. It's on the first floor of an old renovated

Malmi

The people of Malmi work in modern offices and chop wood for the sauna under the shade of lilac trees. There are families where as many as three generations have attended the same schools and whose former teachers are well remembered in the area. Nowadays, these schools are part of Helsinki's huge educational system. At some of them not even one out of ten of the teachers lives in Malmi. Private shopkeepers stubbornly survive alongside the supermarkets and ever encroaching chainstores. New times may crush the homely corner foodstores, but not the florists, goldsmiths and watchmakers, small dress stores, photographers. Malmi born-and-bred cobblers, or the bookshop dating from the 1920s. Such entrepreneurs still have the knack and take time to chat with their customers while wrapping their purchases, to the super stores few shoppers say anything to the friendly check-out girls. A school from the 1920s and Kristian Gullichsen's church from 1981 face each other across the four-lane road – the centuries old highway to Hame.   >

Helsinki competing in the world

At the beginning of 1997 there were 532 800 people living in Helsinki. As the annual increase is estimated at 4 400, by 2000 the population will be 547 000 and by 2015 about 575 000.

Compared to the postwar period, the city is ever more interested in highly-educated youth. Nationwide migration to the larger conurbations has brought people to the greater metropolitan area. Helsinki considers the capital's dynamicism beneficial, if not indispensable, to the whole nation.

On the rim of Helsinki

>20

■ MANNERHEIMINTIE,
  THE MAIN ROUTE TO THE NORTH

■ OLD STUDENT HOUSE

■ PARLIAMENT BUILDING
  MUSEUM OF CONTEMPORARY
  ART, KIASMA

■ NUMEROUS PASSAGES
  UNDER THE ROAD CONNECT
  DEPARTMENT STORES AND
  THE METRO

■ THREE SMITHS' SQUARE

13

■ STUDENT THEATRE

■ CITY PASSAGE

■ TALLBERG'S HOUSE

ALEKSANTERINKATU
TOWARDS SENATE SQUARE,
THE MARKET SQUARE AND
HELSINKI UNIVERSITY'S
MAIN BUILDING
■

■ STOCKMANN'S
DEPARTMENT
STORE

■

THE THREE SMITHS STATUE,
Felix Nylund, 1932

15

MANNERHEIMINTIE TO THE
SOUTH
■

■ PRIMULA CORNER

■ KALEVANKATU

■ THREE SMITHS' SQUARE

Aarne Laurila

The Helsinki of the
Helsinkians

Helsinkians combine internationalism with Finnish-ness. Weather permitting, they enjoy pavement cafés like the French and Italians, or the Viennese and Budapestians. They long for the pubs familiar from London and Prague and get them, too many of them some say. Like the Americans they have learned to spend their time in department stores, shopping malls and hypermarkets the size of football fields where it's always warm. They buy the evening papers almost mechanically. They control the northern climate by ex-tending the short summers in swimming halls and roller skiing when there's no snow. Summer only interrupts the ice hockey season by two or three months, and hockey promoters had no difficulty in commissioning a 13 250-seat stadium. Even culture bugs were inveigled into participating by forecasts of using the Hartwall Stadium for mega-concerts. After all, Pavarotti, Placido Domingo, Kiri Te Kanawa, Harry Belafonte and Frank Sinatra had appeared at the old Ice Hall, and even Pope John II had held a service there.   >

● But Helsinki is there where it is. The first and last matches of the soccer season are normally played in icy rains or snowstorms, with only some 500-1000 shivering spectators in attendance. Winter divides Helsinkians. Some yearn for the white snows and cold brilliance of the countryside. Such people enjoy skiing in the parks and recreation grounds. Others submit uncomplainingly to the damp greyness typical of the southern coast where the temperature hovers around zero. Spring, however, unites them. April's melting snows mostly irritate mums with small kids but by early May at the latest - apart from those allergic to the flowering and leafing of limes and maples - all stop to gaze wistfully at the sea, at its nuances and immutability. Throughout the year, but most intensely in summer, Helsinkians feel a closeness to some park, wood or individual tree. As the weekend approaches queues of cars stream out towards the countryside - uniting great numbers of people. The summer house exodus continues until the end of autumn. Town dwellers visit the markets, sit in the parks and gardens, sail to nearby islands or far into the open sea, fish from a bridge or the mouth of the River Vantaa, the Mother of Helsinki. They know that the fish market opens at the beginning of October, when dozens of fishing boats moor alongside the Market Square. They have come from the coastal regions of the Gulfs of Finland and Bothnia, from the Åland Islands and Estonia. Salted and spiced fish, home-made bread and handicrafts are bought and sold.

Airline passengers see Helsinki as part of the coast of the Gulf of Finland. You can only recognise the city if you know the place. From the sea Helsinki slowly emerges into view. To the traveller on the lookout for land it's like an unfolding play. Those arriving by train or car pass through the transformation of Helsinki: first comes the sparsely populated countryside fractured by busy motorways, then the suburbs of dormitory towns, industrial estates, shopping centres, clusters of little houses, high-class architecture and the absence of architectural sense.

A town should be such that its inhabitants feel it to be their own. That's what they say. Helsinkians' feel that Parliament Building, the Council of State, the buildings of the University of Helsinki scattered throughout the city, the Bank of Finland, Finlandia Hall, the Olympic Stadium, the National Theatre, the new Opera House built in 1994, Zoo Island, Linnanmäki Amusement Park and Stock-

mann's department store are national buildings, although each and everyone of them has a personal relationship. Stockmann's is the only place common to all generations of Helsinkians; Senate Square, the neoclassical heart of Helsinki, is not a place where all age groups congregate at the same time. The Cathedral towering above Senate Square is national, Temppeliaukio Church is for tourists and music lovers, the other churches, ranging from the Old Church designed by Carl Ludwig Engel to the modern ones in the suburbs, are for Helsinkians. Townfolk enjoy a quiet stroll down Bulevardi, passing the Old Church, the former opera house, the Sinebrychoff Art Museum of old foreign masters, numerous affluent commercial and residential buildings with cafés, art galleries, boutiques and antique stores at street level, but not, thank goodness, a single supermarket. The seasoned

Helsinkian enjoys the vistas opening from the foyer of the Swedish Theatre or over Eläintarhanlahti Bay from the entrance of the City Theatre, the second of the two bays which dominate the milieu of the city centre. Helsinkians revere Eila Hiltunen's Sibelius Monument, so beloved by tourists, but also the birch trees growing in the park named after the composer, and where the Helsinki of Finland and Helsinkians overlaps. That fragment of mid-1930s functionalism, Lasipalatsi - Glass Palace, was formerly a landmark for country folk, helping them to find the bus station. For townsfolk it meant the Rex Cinema, a number of established shops and an historic ice cream bar.

The history we acquired

The town which King Gustav Vasa of Sweden founded in 1550 at the mouth of the River Vantaa on the north coast of the Gulf of Finland has no spiritual association with the majority of Helsinkians. It is not the custom to visit there looking for memorials or the ruins of the first

church. This peaceful place is dominated by wooden houses, lilacs and maples. In 1640, the regency government of Queen Christina decided to move the tenuously developing town from this low-lying area a few kilometres south to the Vironniemi headland. When considering the number of visible memories of times past, Helsinki cannot compare to Turku, the former capital, let alone Viipuri in which the centuries from the middle ages to the 1930s have survived. Finland lost Viipuri to the Soviet Union in the second world war. Together with the other displaced Carelians, the people of that bustling cultural and commercial city settled in Finland, very many of them in Helsinki.

From the 18th century are Sederholm House on the corner of Senate Square, the oldest stone building in mainland Helsinki and nowadays a museum, and that part of the island fortress outside the city built by the Swedes, originally called Sveaborg or Sweden's castle, but renamed after independence Suomenlinna or Finland's castle. The Russians extended the fortifications during the 19th century. Having lost its geopolitical importance, Suomenlinna has become one of four UNESCO cultural heritage sites in Finland. Its historic milieu and nature inspires people to paint, draw, perform boisterous plays, or just sit and enjoy themselves. It can be freezing cold on Suomenlinna, but on a sunny day warm enough to swim off the craggy coastline. Small boys and even energetic girls clamber over the ancient guns or squeeze themselves inside the museum submarine Vesikko; the last of the line for Finland no longer has submarines. Other visitors to Suomenlinna remember the Reds imprisoned here in 1918 by the victorious Whites after the bitter civil war.

In 1812, a few years after Russia had taken Finland from Sweden, Tsar Alexander I made Helsinki the capital of the new autonomous grand duchy because the old capital Turku was slightly too near the former motherland. During the 19th century churches, ministries, the university, commercial houses, the House of Estates, the Ateneum Art Museum, the fire station, Kaivohuone restaurant and the Market Hall were erected in Helsinki. These

constitute the essence of Helsinki. But of the factories built then, those instruments of power and providers of sustenance, few traces remain. The low and high tenements where the poor lived have also been destroyed. In Kallio and Sörnäinen, to the north of the old centre, a few stalwart buildings remain as evidence of working class endeavours at the turn of the century. By establishing housing companies workers' families secured a home for themselves as well as roots in the city. For those with money and time - and few had - visits were paid to their former homes in Pohjanmaa, Häme and Savo. Long holidays were beyond the wildest dreams of most.

The building of the centre in the 19th century raised the civic pride of Helsinkians. Similar fine buildings were erected as in the famous towns of the older European states. Riitta Nikula in her essay discusses the work of the young architects who, at the turn of the century, also wished to introduce national characteristics into their work. The relationship of Helsinkians to their town became richer. The country set its sights on full independence and the buildings of the capital confirmed a belief in Finland's strength.

In the same way Helsinki had faith in the young republic established on 6th December 1917. Finnish architects adopted an independent stance towards international styles. Between the wars the business life of the capital diversified, but it's growth remained under control and a social conscience ensured that no major seats of discontent developed. Housing production was much helped by enterprising working-class ventures to which the town gave its support. Although class boundaries existed, the majority of Helsinkians felt the city as their own.

Helsinki starts to break-up

The war between Finland and the Soviet Union as well as Great Britain ended in September 1944. About a month later, on the same October day that Colonel-General A.A. Zhdanov, head of the Allied Control Commission, arrived in Helsinki under the armistice to take up residence at Hotel Torni in the city centre, the Council of State decided on a number of district mergers: the borough of Haaga, the municipalities of Huopalahti, Oulunkylä and Kulosaari, as well as a horseshoe-shaped chunk from

the Helsinki Rural District were joined to Helsinki. On 1.1.1946 the population of the city rose from 290 000 to 340 000 and its area quintupled. Forests, fields and hills and smallish planned built-up areas, as well as many villages, which had grown freely to the north of Helsinki and alongside the west-bound railway, were joined to the city. During the preceding decades thousands of people had found work in Helsinki, but not a place to live. Some 10 to 15 kilometres from the centre sites were available for those wishing to build their own houses. And for those who could not afford to, there were attics and outhouses to rent. The journey to work was made by train and from the 1920s onwards by coach. Privately and cooperatively-owned stores sprang up in the villages.

There were also workshops, as well as quite considerable factories and warehouses. The village roads were largely cared for by private maintenance companies, water came from garden wells and sewage went where it went.

As new Helsinkians, the inhabitants of the annexed areas expected the services and activities that belong to normal urban life, but first Helsinki had to carry through the difficult task of town planning and the construction of new residential areas. Only a few buildings had been destroying in the bombing of Helsinki. The men were returning from the front and young couples needed flats. People from the countryside came to Helsinki to work and study, and in addition there was the problem of resettling the Carelian evacuees. Wooden buildings were demolished in the working-class districts of Punavuori and Kallio to make way for new blocks of flats, considerable new building went on in the more middle-class area of Töölö, but mostly the town directed its attention to the surrounding lands which it had farsightedly purchased some time before. Traditionally, the town had gradually extended itself beyond its borders so that Helsinkians could feel each new piece as part of a familiar whole. Now was the time of the suburbs.

The new suburbs that sprang up rapidly in the 1950s and 1960s, partly thanks to element con-struction technology, like Herttoniemi, Myllypuro, Roihuvuori, Kontula, Jakomäki, Pihlajamäki, Maunula, North Haaga and Munkkivuori, were quite new communities for Finns. The cream of the country's architects planned them, making a sincere effort to meet the everyday needs of their residents, but for many it meant agonising years waiting for shops, day-care centres, schools and public transport. The reading public were served by libraries on wheels, and the network of health stations and centres that now encompasses Helsinki was only just being conceived.

As each house was completed in the new suburbs, the families moved in, sometimes thousands of them within a few weeks. Even generally speaking the way of life in these suburbs has been criticised and their concrete grimness commented on. They were, however, the only realistic way of housing the needy masses; some of them were built more densely than originally intended, and Helsinki's suburbs were often thought of as the first homes for the rural migrants. In reality many of the younger generation of Helsinkians moved into them at the beginning of their independent life, as well as adults wanting a new home. Many recall their delight at the spaciousness of the flats and their proximity to nature. Forests replaced the absent parks and sand quarries became the new playgrounds.

The movement of thousands of people unknown to each other into often unfinished areas was not without its adjustment problems, but gradually they took the new estates to their hearts. For flat buyers it had meant, and continued to mean, strict saving. This sometimes decades-long sacrifice also meant being bound to the area. Tenants organised themselves. Through voluntary action playgrounds, ski tracks, ice rinks and ball-game pitches were built in the suburbs. Before the introduction of the general nine-year comprehensive school, children normally spent four years at an elementary school before some of them went on to the eight-year grammar school leading to university entrance. But there were no grammar schools in the suburbs so the more active residents founded them. Wastepaper was collected and bazaars held to raise funds for a host of good causes. Church congregations assembled in temporary premises to begin with. Social problems simmered and erupted, but sports clubs, branches of the Mannerheim Child Protection Association and the Red Cross, the Scouts and the Martta women's institutes were established. Branches of the political parties were also set-up and in due course also of the Lions Club. These industrially-constructed suburbs developed into quite unique communities. In the final decade of the 20th century these suburbs, now 30 to 40 year old, were overhauled, apartment blocks were refurbished, shopping centres modernised and the surroundings made more amenable. Second, even third generations of families are now living in the same suburb, the former children and young adults.

Industrial change has also shattered the traditional concept of Helsinki. Downtown, multi-storey factories proved unsuitable for modern production technology and transportation became congested. Sites were provided for industry in new areas, but both land and opportunities were more abundant beyond the city's boundaries. At the same time as factories, warehouses and offices were being erected, residential areas also arose in the neighbouring municipalities. The most famous of these is Tapiola in Espoo. Some twenty years after the war Finland no longer had a clearly definitive capital, but a greater metropolitan area consisting of Helsinki, Espoo, Vantaa and Kauniainen. Although these four towns collaborate over public transport, water and waste management, and operate an inter-library borrowing service, each remains responsible for community planning. Car traffic has consumed land and mutilated the landscape. Internal migration is brisk. But moving to a neighbouring town or within the same town is always somewhat traumatic.

The city closes its ranks again

Helsinki began to take counter measures when migration, in addition to removing people and industry, also decentralised head offices and government bureaus. Even the disappearance of industry was unable to stem the scarcity of sites, so offices were being directed to Pasila, some three kilometres from the centre. Pasila also allowed Helsinki to stop the take-over by offices of prime areas in the city. Government bureaus, head offices, the Finnish Broadcasting Company, the central library and various associations all moved to Pasila. A new Exhibition Centre was built to replace the old one in Töölö, familiar as the venue for mass meetings, dances, revivalist gatherings, boxing matches, war booty exhibitions, veteran reunions and Red Army Choir concerts in addition to fairs. Pasila's historic wooden railway station was jacked up and moved, given to the peace movement and renamed Peace Station. Between Pasila's gaunt buildings pedestrian paths cross over the ground-level roads for cars and trams. The earlier verdant suburb had given way to a very densely urban settlement.

The densely-built East Pasila and the smaller and softer residential West Pasila rapidly filled up. Since the 1960s, quite ordinary apartment blocks had been built in Kulosaari, Oulunkylä and Haaga which, for instance, often blend harmoniously with the existing historic and often refined milieus, but not always. The city, which since the great mergers has gained only Vantaa's Vuosaari in 1966, began to intensive housing along the main railway line. Alongside small houses, and often in place of them, towering blocks of flats were erected. The heritage of local villages crumbled under the impact.

At the same time Helsinki, Vantaa and Espoo began developing the idea of powerful district centres. To the west Espoo decided to strengthen Tapiola and completely modernise Leppävaara. Vantaa began to build up Tikkurila around the old framework. And in the east of Helsinki, a concentration of commercial services took shape in Itäkeskus - East Centre, in which educational and spiritual values were focussed in the Stoa House of Culture and St. Matthew's Church, and physical enjoyment in the fine new swimming baths. To create the northeastern centre, Malmi was fundamentally redesigned. Of these district centres, Tapiola is completely dependent upon car transportation. Itäkeskus is connected to the centre and neighbouring suburbs by the metro. The development of Malmi, Tikkurila and the unfinished Leppävaara has largely relied on the railway. Trains to Tikkurila from the centre via Pasila and Malmi run as frequently as the metro. These connections have united all parts of Helsinki. The capital has become more compact by building new settlements alongside the old ones in Katajanokka, Ruoholahti, and a postmodern Little Huopalahti.

Many types of Helsinkians

Helsinki City Council has approved an internationalisation strategy and has an international meeting place Caisa, but its attitude is ultimately up to the people themselves. Helsinkians are accustomed to the hotel-

■

The kilometre long Pitkäkoski on the border of Helsinki and Vantaa was still a wilderness at the turn of the century. Once the outdoor life and swimming baths became fashionable in the 1920s, swimming and picnic trips could be made to more distant places.

23

sized Swedish ferries, dense air traffic and fast communications. Many international companies have set up their offices here and the World Trade Centre has its premises in Pauli E. Blomstedt's Union Bank House from 1929, one of the finest commercial buildings in modern Helsinki. Cafeterias sell Pizza Slices not slices of something Finnish. Store announcements are also made in Russian for the convenience of shoppers from that country. Chinese and Vietnamese restaurants are as much a part of the scene as American-style hamburger joints and traditional Russian restaurants; the ethnic restaurants have thrived, even during the recession. But not all Asian and African immigrants, Turks and Kurds, or the more recently arrived Russians are treated with equal openness. By the mid-1990s, some five per cent of Helsinkians had a foreign background, and by

2005 it is reckoned to rise to seven per cent.

Finnish and Swedish-speaking Helsinkians are accustomed to living alongside each other, and the tiny Jewish community has made a valuable contribution to the city's cultural and business life. By 1996 the Swedish-speakers accounted for only seven per cent of the population. Their importance and respect has not prevented a fall in this percentage. In their everyday lives almost all of them are bilingual and the Finnish majority has drawn each new generation closer to its own language. The Swedish Theatre and Little Theatre, which often present plays in both languages, have also been successful in appealing to the Finnish-speaking public. Such Swedish-language writers as Tove Jansson, Bo Carpelan, Märta Tikkanen, Christer Kihlman, Jörn Donner, Ralf Nordgren and Kjell Westö have an important following among Finnish-speaking readers. If their works were only published in Swedish they would remain largely unknown to the

Finnish majority. The slang common to the older generation of Helsinkians, the city's social dialect, is to a considerable extent based on Swedish. The young generation, who have America on their minds and English on their tongues, use the new Finnish slang expressions.

Once the idea was launched of making Helsinki one of the cultural cities of Europe for the year 2000, people expressed their wishes in a number of spontaneous initiatives, such as erecting an Arch of Triumph, planting berry forests, a world exhibition, a kite-flying festival, establishing an all-night library and more fancy dress balls. It was also suggested that some order be brought to the shamble of shop advertising, that all buildings be decorated with broad colourful ribbons and that environmentally-unsuitable buildings be demolished - the list of which ranged from Finlandia Hall and the Opera House to the pretentious business premises.

Helsinkians seek their experiences from watching Thunder in Helsinki car racing and classical music concerts, a respect for nature and scribbling graffiti on rock faces, rock music mega-concerts and taking the dog for a quiet walk. Only a wall - admittedly a high stone wall - separates the Hietaniemi cemetery from the city's most popular beach at Hietaranta, where new students with their proud certificates and white caps celebrate into the late spring hours; earlier in the day they had laid roses to the fallen heroes of the 1939-1945 wars. The majority of the audiences of the National Theatre and City Theatre are different from the smaller theatres founded by the younger generation. Some seek and others shun experimental art, architecture, dance. And to many they mean nothing at all.

All Helsinki is proud of its trams. Any change that threatens a park or traditional hospital gets people organised and most believe it was the recession that put an end to plans to demolish the Tennis Palace from the 1930s; the offices and tennis courts are being converted into an ethnographic and art museum and a cinema complex. The relationship between the statue of Mannerheim and the Contemporary Art Museum, and the modernistic statues of presidents Paasikivi, Ryti and Relander, and the writer Mika Waltari are subjects of intense argument. Gradually these controversial subjects will become mere details in the pluristic scene, as have the memorial in Hakaniemi donated by the Soviet

Union and the stiff statues of presidents Svinhufvud, Ståhlberg and Kallio standing guard outside Parliament Building.

A city's prestige

"People only become dignified if they are given a prestigious background," said the Italian professor Giancarlo de Carlo in Helsinki in November 1996. What about Helsinki's worth to its citizens? This depends on the answers to such questions as can I find work and a place to live, will my child receive good day care, does the school come up to my expectations, can I easily get into a good hospital if necessary, and can I spend by old age in safety, but also on what my environment is like and how do cultures meet in my town - meet or pass each other.

A feeling of being a Helsinkian is relatively young. Very few families have lived in the town for even a century; in this respect Helsinki differs from most other European towns. But although migration brings and removes, and Helsinki like any other place in the world is in the throes of continuous change, the town seeks and creates its own character. The number of native-born Helsinkians is rising all the time. The new generations demand, and know how to demand, ever more from the town to which they belong.

Just at the time when Helsinki is becoming more closely tied to the rest of Europe, the town is converting the derelict shore near the famous Arabia Porcelain Factory into a housing estate. The factory continues to operate in part of the building, the rest of which is now the University of Art and Design and the Pop & Jazz Conservatory. All within a few hundred metres of the memorials to the foundation of Helsinki. Gustav Vasa established this new coastal town to compete with Tallinn in Estonia. Now, in the old cloth mill, there is an Art and Communications School for 300 students. Helsinki's ancient history and new future live in mutual harmony. ●

SENATE SQUARE IS THE OLD NEOCLASSICAL CENTRE OF HELSINKI AND WAS DESIGNED BY CARL LUDVIG ENGEL.

27

COUNCIL OF
STATE PALACE

KATAJANOKKA
SHIPPING TERMINAL

PRESIDENTIAL
PALACE

SOUTH HARBOUR

MARKET SQUARE

OLYMPIA TERMINAL

KAIVOPUISTO
PARK

OLD MARKET HALL

■ MIKAEL AGRICOLA CHURCH

■ EROTTAJA FIRE STATION

■ WEST HARBOUR

■ EROTTAJA

■ THE CATHEDRAL, FORMERLY NICHOLAS' CHURCH, WAS ONE OF C.L. ENGEL'S MAIN WORKS. CONSECRATED IN 1852, THE CATHEDRAL WAS FUNDAMENTALLY RESTORED IN 1996-97.

■   STOCKMANN'S DEPARTMENT STORE

■   HOTEL TORNI

■ STREET REFLECTIONS
KATARIINANKATU AND SOFIANKATU

■ NORTH ESPLANADE, KATARIINANKATU AND SOFIANKATU   ■   SOFIANKATU

■   KATARIINANKATU

HELSINKI CITY
EXECUTIVE BOARD
IN SEPTEMBER 1996.
WOMEN OCCUPY THE
THREE LEADING
POSTS.

MARKET SQUARE

EXCURSIONS INTO HELSINKI, TIME AND PLACE

Riitta Nikula

1.
Cycling on a summer's night

As you approach Helsinki from the west in the early morning dawn, the new cycle path leads you to a serene bygone idyll in Lauttasaari beside the broad lanes of a motorway. Two tiny red cabins perched on the rocky shore are all that remains of the simple fisherman's life in these coastal waters. They faithfully stand guard to the forest of aluminium masts that opens up before them. >

● Astonishingly, on the marina embankment, are the first intimations of Senate Square, for among the soil and rubble are moss-covered stone blocks from the facade of the former Pohjoismaiden Osakepankki bank on Unioninkatu built in 1904. Fragments of the floral and fauna motifs hewn to the drawings of Herman Gesellius, Armas Lindgren and Eliel Saarinen now lie in a jigsaw puzzle confusion. You'll have to check the drawings to see whether the halo of headless doves belonged to the deep arch over the main entrance or the impressive oriel in the middle of the smooth facade, which disappeared when the building was demolished in 1934 to make way for a massive, monstrous and cheerless granite palace.

The narrow path meandering along the shores of Lauttasaari has to be peddled with care. The stony surface is slippery and people are still sleeping in their summer chalets. You wonder whether it wouldn't be possible for people to spend their private and public leisure in such harmony elsewhere? Passersby delight in the beauty of the little gardens and so respect the privacy of these unfenced chalets. The rocks and sea are there for all to enjoy.

A few twists and turns later the verdant scene changes into a townscape of terrace houses from the Fifties and low apartment blocks from the following decade. The cosy detailed, mainly white-plastered architecture changes surreptitiously into an ominous affluence. Posh cars line the narrow roads. The owners are still asleep.

Beyond the beach a flank of massive apartment blocks appears on the south point of Lauttasaari, the first reminder of the victory of rationalism over aestheticism in home building. Many good flats, but precious little architectural joy.

Over Lauttasaari bridge the bold outline of industrial Ruoholahti stands against the pale horizon and emphasises the flaming shape of Martti Aiha's Rumba sculpture; quite flabbergasting in this light and silence, before the cars and trams choke the view. The city at night offers unique experiences, the different light, silence and coolness transpose you from the ordinary.

At the entrance to the Cable Factory cultural and art centre posters flutter in the morning breeze. Already some people are going to work, but others are just now going home to bed. It seems that the blocks of flats in still unfinished Ruoholahti have come ever closer to the factories. There's still plenty of embanking and building to do. When it's ready, the last vestiges of the old harbour and small-scale industry will have disappeared, stable conditions have then supplanted the quaint

■ WEST HARBOUR

■
MARTTI AIHA'S RUMBA SCULPTURE IN FRONT OF A STUDENTS' DORMITORY (1992) IN RUOHOLAHTI

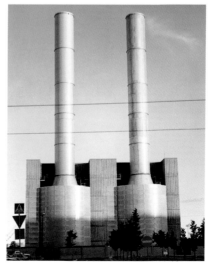

■ RUOHOLAHTI

■ TELAKKAKATU

transitoriness and mood of continuous change that I have enjoyed for over twenty years. Will any of the strange plants that grew in such profusion on the shore, their seeds borne by ships from unknown lands, find their way into the new gardens? Hopefully, the Cable Factory will retain its character for it cannot survive excessive refinement or wanton order.

Ruoholahti canal is beautiful. Architect Juhani Pallasmaa's firm grasp of the architecture of the embankments and bridges has lightened the expression of the massive blocks of houses. Pekka Helin's Laivapoika (cabinboy) apartment block acts as a gateway closing the eastern end of the area. Its eloquent outline dominates the traffic to West Harbour and the great ships in the Hietalahti dockyard. This new neighbourhood has confidently taken its place on the map of Helsinki. The building of Ruoholahti began in 1991, and within a few years it will provide a home for some 9000 and work for about 5000 people.

Even now it is difficult to imagine that the docklands of Jätkäsaari and Munkkisaari will be part of residential Helsinki in the coming decades. For the people of Helsinki, its harbours have always a breathing space. Even looking at ships is now restricted, for fences and guards prohibit people from their traditional Sunday promenades.

■

WORK ON THE RESIDENTIAL AREA OF RUOHOLAHTI ALMOST IN THE MIDDLE OF HELSINKI BEGAN IN 1991.

To compensate for this seaport ambience, townsfolk have been placated with such monumental embankments that the residents of Eira and Ullanlinna have publicly protested the destruction of the mysterious nooks and crannies of their childhood. On a beautiful weekend it seems as though all Finland comes here to promenade. On a sunny winter's day, when the ice supports but the snow's not too deep, there's a joyful exodus to the isles of Sirpalesaari, Liuskaluoto, Uunisaari and Harakka. Spellbound by the vast openness, even strangers smile at each other. So long as the ice road is open, the hardy walkers trek to Suomenlinna for coffee. Now as dawn breaks on this early summer's morn, Merikatu and the sea front are strangely deserted. The boats are at their moorings, but the strollers sleep on.

The carpet-washing jetty at the end of Ehrensvärdintie waits for the waters to warm. How long will the carpet washers tolerate being a side-show for busloads of gawking tourists? In few places do such ordinary chores provide such innocent amusement for the curious. Art students could dream up many a performance to stage on this theme.

It's fun watching the market come to life in South Harbour. The stalls are soon up, but stocking them takes longer. The first hum of traffic can be heard, and by seven in the summer the first shoppers will appear. In winter's wet and gloom the number of stallholders seems to diminish with each passing year.

Who can they sell too in an empty market? It is just here that you realise how tightly Finland is bound to the seasons. In summer you can't get into a coffee tent however long you queue. In winter the most faithful are the fishmongers and their regular customers. Not even the Swedish ferries will save the bigger markets in winter, although the renaissance of Esplanade may largely be due to them. Refined cafés and Finnish Design are not at the mercy of the elements.

MIKAEL AGRICOLA
CHURCH AND THE
DISTRICT OF EIRA

No Helsinki brochure can fail to feature the Market Square and its superb location, with the sea in front and a row of historic palaces in the background. Engel's Seurahuone hotel, which since the 1910s has served as Helsinki's City Hall, and Heidenstrauch's palace, refurbished in the 1920s as the Swedish embassy and somewhat resembling the royal palace in Stockholm, both draw your attention. In the middle of the market stands the Tsarina's Stone, an obelisk surmounted by a bronze double-headed eagle, offering the first hint of a third, oriental flavour, for to the right in the distance, on Katajanokka's highest point, rises the Byzantine brick edifice of Uspenski Cathedral.

The brand new cycle path winds along Katajanokka Canal in front of the warehouses beneath Uspenski Cathedral and on to the Pohjoisranta waterfront. Here you can view the cathedral in all its glory, whereas from South Harbour and the Market Square its enchantment is obscured by the strict cubism of the Carrara marble faced Enzo-Gutzeit head office designed by Alvar Aalto in the 1960s. It was then thought a perfect solution for the milieu as it gained its proportion from the buildings on North Esplanade.

Not all old Helsinkians like the granite embankment on Pohjoisranta as it has moved the waterfront further from the houses. Others approve as it facilitates the flow of traffic from the east. The old firewood quay has become a mooring for historic wooden ships, which are so wonderful to look at. For marine history enthusiasts this is an ideal place in summer as you can see the fleet of rugged icebreakers in its summer mooring in front of Engel's classical Merikasarmi building. Seen from another side, you could imagine that the stream of foreign visitors to the Ministry for Foreign Affairs, which Merikasarmi now houses, will soon manage to put Helsinki and Finland on the map. There's no need to go further to find subjects for small talk.

The romanticism of Pohjoisranta clashes violently with the stark concrete rationalism of Merihaka. This massive complex of high-rise apartment blocks gazes severely over the historically stratified districts of Kruunun-haka and Katajanokka and also conceals the former industrial milieu of

■ THE URSA OBSERVATORY
IN KAIVOPUISTO

■ KAIVOPUISTO PARK HAS FUNCTIONED AS HELSINKI'S
LARGEST CONCERT HALL SINCE THE 1980s.

Sörnäisten Rantatie. It is a constant reminder of the planning optimism of the 1960s and 1970s, of extreme functionalism, according to which reason and a bit of money would provide the answer to all ordinary human needs. In those days, when few cared for humble tales of old towns, building conservationists took their first hesitant steps and suffered their first bitter defeats.

The industrial architecture of Kone ja Silta (later Wärtsilä) almost disappeared without trace from Sörnäisten Rantatie, but in recent decades the rather homely Näkinpuisto residential estate has grown up on the site. Already a couple of head offices have moved to cheaper addresses from the now listed separator factory, but nobody will dare destroy Armas Lindgren's red-brick architecture after its expensive renovation. The same is to be hoped for its cousin, the warehouse Väinö Vähäkallio designed for OTK, whose gaunt closed walls contain such amusing motifs.

Once traditional industry disappears from the centre of a city, factory chimneys no longer belch smoke, and there is no need for the miscellaneous buildings of industry, then the built up city is threatened with impoverishment. If, in addition to a few cultural and administrative monuments, only offices and department stores provide work in the stone city, life becomes very anaemic. Why can't industrial blocks be gradually converted into ingenious dwellings?

■

USPENSKI CATHEDRAL AND THE KATAJANOKKA WAREHOUSES

■

C.L. ENGEL'S MERIKASARMI IS NOWADAYS HOME TO THE MINISTRY FOR FOREIGN AFFAIRS

The sensitive lines of the concrete architecture of Suvilahti gasworks are the result of Selim A. Lindqvist's design from 1908-13. Fortunately, the building has been so many times declared of value that, well cared for, it can expect a new use at the corner of the motorway east. I wonder if Lindqvist's gasometre will be allowed to remain in the same company? Perhaps it will be appreciated as an environmental work of art, now that the jolly ideas of young artists have made town dwellers conscious of their surroundings. In summer 1993 interest focussed on the coal stacks alongside Sörnäisten Ranta-tie when lupines and rye grass were planted for the hares to feed on. When winter came they dug holes in the coal to warm their backsides. Only their heads could be seem poking out from the stacks.

■

ICEBREAKERS MOORED OFF KATAJANOKKA (IN THE FOLDER)

Itäväylä, the eastern motorway, so bisects the island of Kulosaari that motorists never realise that, apart from a few odd shaped wood villas, Finland's first garden city was founded here in 1907. The cycle path turns south to meet the old coastal road. Taking the northern route you come to the small island cemetery of Leposaari with Armas Lindgren's chapel, probably the smallest in the country. There are memorials to the garden city pioneers who, at the beginning of the century, sought a new way of life.

■   POHJOISRANTA

The cycle path turns into the verdant suburb of Herttoniemi. From the high rocks a view opens over the Old City bay, behind which are the neat rows on the shores of Toukola and Vanhakaupunki. Much empty space, the Arabia buildings seem so small that you wonder how they could house all the faculties of the University of Art and Design. The Viikki nature conservation area is spacious and green, the farm fields still in their dark spring hues.

Postwar West Herttoniemi is a soft composition of residential buildings in many shapes and sizes. Detached houses are a variation on the one-and-a-half storey theme, terrace houses with lush back gardens line the curving roads. Tower blocks stand proudly on the highest rocks and emphasise everything which the planners valued in the surrounding nature. Many foundations are faced in decorative slate compositions, firmly binding the soft-coloured buildings to the bedrock.

The postwar need to take root, "heroic materialism", now comes to mind. Throughout the world exhibitions are held of the art and architecture of the 1950s. A couple of decades ago this was derided as sentimental tinkering. If only you knew how long it takes before derision becomes fond love, you could set a suitable period of time for the protection of all new buildings. This would avoid pointless arguments and avoid the evil of hasty judgements.

 MERIHAKA

■ HERTTONIEMI

Everything is huge in Itäkeskus. The new commercial centre designed by Erkki Kairamo, the Maamerkki landmark from 1987, can be seen from far away, first above the woods, and closer behind the blocks of red-brick buildings. The new shopping mall on Itäväylä, thumped down at the end of the earlier one, is the largest in Scandinavia. The oldest shopping centre in the area, Puotinharju built in the 1960s, which looked so impressive at one time, is now almost impossible to recognise within this new dimension. The central arcade of the new shopping paradise lies under a glass barrel vault, the interior divided by pillars of steel, water splashes and there is space enough for indoor plants in this

■ BIOTECHNOLOGY AT VIIKKI

55

eternal summer. Juhani Pallasmaa's architecture battles with the cacophony of cheap emporia.

On the other side of Itäväylä the intense blue of Hannu Sirén's Stoa sculpture steadies the nerves. There's always something interesting happening at the cultural centre, even if it's only new books and records in the library. Across the quiet courtyard, the small church designed by Björn Krogius and Veli-Pekka Tuominen offers the cosy sanctuary of a village church in a new way. Of all the new areas, Itäkeskus most resembles a town, densely built and effective, but also in its own way curious and exciting because of the variety of different elements.

Further to the east Vuosaari is being built beyond recognition. The loosely-woven suburb built by home-savers in the 1960s is now divided into numerous clusters of neighbourhoods, whose new shopping centre shocks with its streams of shoppers. The apartment blocks of this decade show a preference for enclosed courtyards and soft pastel colours. The myriad details have quite obviously been designed just for the fun of it, as a natural reaction to the stark monotony of early suburbs like Kontula and Myllypuro. The residents of Vuosaari have a more mixed national background than those in any other part of Helsinki. The new spirit of the architecture is in harmony with the exceptional everyday. ●

■ MERI-RASTILA

The Helsinki, the planning and building of which began in 1812 on the order and under the personal supervision of Tsar Alexander I as the capital of his new autonomous grand duchy, was the creation of the Swedish courtier, Albert Ehrenström, and Carl Ludvig Engel, a Prussian architect seasoned via St. Petersburg and Tallinn. Both were united by the prevailing European style, neoclassicism, which enabled Helsinki to be built with the clear message that Russia was a fully-fledged member of the Western world.

2.

The historic layers of the capital

Riitta Nikula

Where the king of Sweden had failed miserably in the 16th century, the emperor of Russia now succeeded beyond all expectations. The Helsinki founded by Gustav Vasa in 1550 at the mouth of the River Vantaa was to have become a powerful competitor to Tallinn, which then controlled trade in the Gulf of Finland. Forced to move from their homes in Ulvila, Rauma, Porvoo and Tammisaari, the new inhabitants were miserable in the new town. They fled back home, thus giving their sovereign a clear message that even the most single-minded town policy has its limits. The grandiose plan for Helsinki was doomed from the outset and today its few remains are even difficult for archaeologists to interpret.   >

59

ONE OF THE OLDEST RESIDENCES
IN HELSINKI, SUOMENLINNA

● Even the Helsinki on the Vironniemi headland was but a small town in the shadow of Sveaborg (nowadays Suomenlinna) built off the coast in the latter half of the 18th century. The fortifications built on six islands under the direction of Augustin Ehrensvärd was the greatest construction project in Swedish history at that time. Thanks to the Franco-Swedish military alliance, the French contributed 67 casks of gold towards its building. Most of the work was done by conscript soldiers who returned to their smallholdings each winter.

The curtain wall on Susisaari contained the Iso Linnanpiha inner bailey, which in its heyday was the most monumental square in Finland. The ingenious false perspective which made the square appear larger than it was, was partly destroyed in the second half of the 19th century, but near the memorial to Augustin Ehrensvärd it is still possible to sense its ceremonial past. King Gustav III himself helped to design the monument.

■

TYKISTÖNLAHTI, SUOMENLINNA

The Helsinki of the Swedish period was destroyed in the fire of 1808 and about a third of the 4000 or so inhabitants lost their homes. Thus the building of the capital could begin with an unusually clean sheet. Johan Albert Ehrenström's town plan, approved in 1817, made Senate Square the centre of Helsinki. Suurkatu, south of the old square, was renamed Aleksanterinkatu in honour of the emperor. The main north-south road was formed by Unioninkatu leading to the square. Ehrenström created a tree-lined avenue between the Esplanades, with the intention of only allowing stone buildings on the north side, permitting wooden houses on the south side as in the other suburban areas. Bulevardi became the main thoroughfare to Hietalahti bay. The Kluuvinlahti bay was filled in to bring uniformity to the grid-plan blocks of the centre.

Following Carl Ludvig Engel's appointed as architect of the recon-struction committee in 1816, he began designing buildings for Senate Square. The first to become completed was the Imperial Senate palace in 1822, nowadays the Council of State, on the east side of the square. Ten years later it received its complement on the opposite side of the square, the main building of the University. One of the finer points of neoclassicism was that the Corinthian columns of the Senate indicated the Roman origins of this institution, whereas the Ionian columns of the University signified that the building belonged to the realm of Apollo, the god of poetry and music. The University Library on the corner of Unioninkatu, which many consider the most beautiful of Engel's numerous public buildings, was not finished until

■ SENAATINTORI
ALEKSANTERINKATU,
COURTYARD

1844. Nicholas' Church, nowadays the Cathedral, which he considered his most important design project of the decades, Engel never saw completed as he died in 1840 and the church was not consecrated until 1852. Engel's ascetic architecture for the church's exterior remained under the corner towers designed by his successor Ernst Bernhard Lohrmann and the statutes of the Apostles he commissioned. These German-made zinc statues darkened and embrittled as time passed and their restoration in 1996-7 was quite an impressive operation.

CHOLERA BASIN, THE DEPARTURE POINT FOR MOTOR BOAT TOURS

In addition to dozens of public buildings, Engel also designed several single-storey wooden dwellings in the suburbs. The best preserved milieu of these pleasant block-type houses is to be found in the new part of Porvoo, the town plan for which Engel drew in the 1830s. His own home and garden was in Bulevardi. As the wealth and population of Helsinki expanded, these wooden houses had to make way for multistorey stone buildings. Their disappearance was considered quite positive until the 1930s when the future professor Nils-Erik Wickberg showed for the first time in his study the uniqueness of neoclassical wooden buildings and wrote in defence of their preservation. In the 1960s two well-preserved wooden buildings were dismantled in Pursimiehenkatu, stored and reassembled in the 1980s in Kaisaniemenranta, beside the University Botanical Gardens.

63

■ SOUTH
HARBOUR   ■ OLD MARKET HALL

S

225°

■ ESPLANADE PARK AND
KAPPELI RESTAURANT

W

330°   N

■ CATHEDRAL

SOFIANKATU PANORAMA

■ CITY HALL

■ KATARIINANKATU

330°

N

40°

160°

S

■ MARKET SQUARE

N 60°10'14"
E 24° 56'40"

BANDSTAND

225°

MARKET SQUARE

E

330°

SOFIANKATU
AND THE CATHEDRAL

■ ESPLANADE, KAPPELI
RESTAURANT

120°

■ SOUTH ESPLANADE

S

■

KATARIINANKATU

■ AT THE OTHER END OF
THE PARK 'THE SWEDISH
THEATRE'

W
270°

310°

■ NORTH ESPLANADE

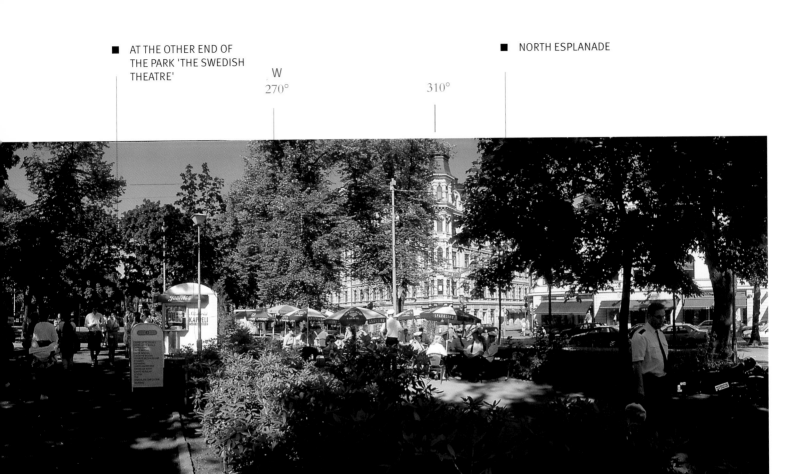

Together with an existing building, they now form a group which most
visitors to the cosy little café in one of them believe is original. Being
fragments of an outdoor museum is perhaps a better alternative than total
destruction when the conflict becomes so escalated, even though it
destroys the authenticity of the townscape. It was not until the 1980s that
the eastern wing was finally added to Engel's Merikasarmi. It had not
been built earlier because the money ran out, and the building's asym-
metry was a living reminder that there are limits even to a tsar's purse.

By the 1880s Helsinki had become quite the metropolis. With a population of a little more than 20 000 in 1860, by 1890 it was over 60 000
and a decade later in excess of 90 000. The townscape changed mostly
through the erection of multistorey blocks of rented apartments. North
Esplanade became Finland's most continental street. The prosperous
bourgeoisie commissioned houses along the lines of Paris, St. Petersburg, Vienna and Berlin, confidently designed by Theodor Höijer, the
most able and popular architect of the time. During a couple of decades,
he designed twelve rentable apartment blocks, whose facades and stair
halls acquired a varied, but mostly profuse decorativeness.

The block-size palace on North Esplanade, commissioned by the
industrialist Fredrik Wilhelm Grönqvist from Höijer, was larger and

more expensive than any other private project undertaken in the country before. A couple of years later he designed on the adjacent site Hotel Kämp, whose luxurious restaurant became the most prominent venue for the leaders of Finnish industry and culture. The building was demolished in the 1960s and replaced by a bank, part of which was in imitation of the old one. In 1996 the decision was taken to rebuild the hotel and restaurant. Fresh winds were blowing. Esplanade, which in the 1960s had declined into gloomy offices and car showrooms, now flourishes with cafés, restaurants and elegant shops competing for the attention of strollers. Fairs and fashion shows are arranged in the park, also concerts, art exhibitions and more or less spontaneous performances.

Theodor Höijer also designed much for industry and public life. The Fire Station on Keskuskatu has been demolished, and with it the legendary Kestikartano restaurant. The sturdy tower of the red-brick Central Fire Station in Korkeavuorenkatu still, however, reminds you of the city hall in Berlin. The branch library in Rikhardinkatu serves inner-city readers in its tastefully restored home and the Ateneum off Railway Square, renamed the National Gallery of Finland in 1990, entices people to its huge exhibitions now that teaching no longer occupies valued space.

■ UNIVERSITY LIBRARY,
THE ROTUNDA,
UNIONINKATU,
Carl Ludwig Engel, 1840

The noblest monumental environment from the last decades of the 19th century was built behind Nicholas' Church. Thanks to the international architectural competition for the Bank of Finland in 1875, the Berliner Ludwig Bohnstedt designed a building on the lines of an Italian Renaissance palace.

Many a competition was held for the House of Estates opposite the Bank completed in 1891, but its interior and exterior is a tribute to the elegant classicism of Gustaf Nyström. The year before he had designed the State Archives diagonally across the road. Its strictly classical composition boldly incorporated new building techniques. Today's genealogists have at their disposal the finest archive room in all Finland, whose exposed iron structures satisfy both the requirements of fire security and lighting. This ultra-modern solution was considered so strange in Finland, that in his defence Nyström stressed its use in the national libraries of London and Paris. For Finland's national library, Engel's university Library, he designed a semi-circular extension in the 1900s, the Rotunda.

At the turn of the century, Nyström's most gifted students at the Polytechnic (since 1908 the University of Technology) revolted against the

classicism of their professor, and through architectural competitions soon managed to put their new ideas into practice. Herman Gesellius, Armas Lindgren and Eliel Saarinen had not even graduated when, in 1897, they won their first competition and designed a new kind of apartment block at Satamakatu 5 in Katajanokka. Commissioned by Julius Tallberg to be built on the front edge of this new district, the four-storey building they designed, asymmetrical and sculptured in form, with a steep roof, corner towers, oriels and a profusion of detail, owed its shape on the one hand to the townscape, and on the other hand to solutions for the interiors of large apartments based on the new housing ideals.

With increasing fervor the young architects studied the historic architecture of their own country and the new stylistic trends in Europe and the United States in order to produce a new, original architecture. Thus the art nouveau inspired by national romanticism is simultaneously national and international. In the case of the National Museum, Gesellius, Lindgren and Saarinen brought about a heated polemic in the press and the subsequent architectural competition of 1902 which they won. Each stylistic period of national culture was expressed in some part of the new museum, and the varied totality was consummated with a narrow tower observable from far off. The dream of an outdoor museum for Hesperia Park was never realised.

■

RAILWAY YARD
FROM LINNUNLAULU
BRIDGE

Katajanokka and Eira, Helsinki's first suburbs, became the main areas for the new style. Following the famous trio, other designers, even master builders, enthused over the new freedom and lyrical decoration. It is for this reason that even Helsinki's fin-de-siecle architecture is so full of nuances. Lars Sonck's Helsinki Telephone Company building in Korkeavuorenkatu and Gesellius, Lindgren and Saarinen's Pohjola Insurance Company building in Aleksanterinkatu are the most succulently sculptured achievements of Helsinki's art nouveau. The architects portrayed the insurance company's functions and name through national-romantic ornamentation, exploiting the hitherto unknown potential of a new facade material, Juuka soapstone. The main entrance is guarded by grimacing gargoyles carved by Hilda Flodin and a bevy of bears. The impressive wood carvings and wrought iron fixtures on the pillars, banisters and doors in the staircase have been interpreted as either the disorders and diseases described in the Kalevala or the misbegotten boys born to serve the Mistress of the North.

In the 1904 competition for a new central railway station there were still many romantic designs, but criticism of the rationalism of Sigurd Frosterus and Gustaf Strengell caused even Eliel Saarinen to develop his winning entry along new lines. As the station gradually emerged in the late 1910s, it was especially admired for its clear spatial arrangement, powerful concrete structures and disciplined overall composition.

CENTRAL RAILWAY
STATION ■

N   20°   E

■ TÖÖLÖ BAY

Lars Sonck adopted a heavy rhythmic symmetry in his Stock Exchange building in Fabianinkatu, the Mortgage Bank building in North Esplanade and the massive warehouse in Katajanokka. In 1912 the working-class district of Kallio received his granite-surfaced church, a landmark seen from all corners of the city. At the end of Siltasaarenkatu, it is the extreme point at one end of Helsinki's longest monumental perspective, the southern point of which is the Observatory designed by Engel in Tähtitorninmäki.

Some of the modest wooden homes on Kallio's Lines dating from the last decades of the 19th century survived into the 1960s. On the more important roads and squares stone apartment blocks had been built from the turn of the century onwards. The district was

■

FINLANDIA HALL,
Alvar Aalto, 1971

■

TÖÖLÖ BAY

160°

S

N 60°10'63"
E 24°56'04"

TELEPHONE TOWER,
PASILA
■

■ THE OLYMPIC
STADIUM

FINNISH NATIONAL
OPERA
■

W

330°

N

■ UNIVERSITY BOTANICAL
GARDENS, KAISANIEMI

planned in parts and it was not until the modern clearance town plan that the old enclosed blocks were finally destroyed and the boundaries and directions defined by monotonous, multi-storey apartment blocks.

Hakaniemi Market Square is framed by different-aged buildings. On the north side are Lars Sonck's red-brick citadel-like Arena building from the 1920s, blending harmoniously with the older market hall. The building of its neighbour, the circular Ympyrätalo from the late-1960s designed by Kaija and Heikki Siren, erased much modest early 20th century architecture. The trade unions' Metallitalo on the south side was built when there was still no discussion of townscape. Encircled by heavy traffic it appears difficult to resuscitate the square, though every so often there are serious attempts to do so.

During its first decade of independence building in Finland first fell to an all time low and then rose to an unprecedented level, whether this is measured in square metres or the number of flats. The indefatigable Bertel Jung, appointed as Helsinki's first town planning architect in 1908, presented his preliminary ideas for a master plan for the city at the beginning of the 1910s, but for the most part they remained on paper. The same fate befell Eliel Saarinen's grandiloquent plan, initially for Munkkiniemi-Haaga, but ultimately for a modern metropolis complete with satellite towns.

One important part of Jung's great idea was, however, realised: Central Park, which brings an unbroken green belt as far as Töölö Bay. He would have liked a fine gateway to mark the entrance to the park and an axel of public buildings, but these remained on paper like other plans for the centre. Due to Saarinen's suggestive perspective drawing, the broad, almost 100 metre long Kuningasavenyy (Kings Avenue) in Jung and Saarinen's Pro Helsingfors plan continues to obsess people. Space could have been made for it by filling in Töölö Bay. Oiva Kallio won the 1925 city centre competition with a design based on similar premises. He spent two years developing the plan, but nothing came of it.

Throughout the whole period of independence, people have dreamed of a new centre for the Töölö Bay area. Since the completion of Parliament Building, planners have viewed the area as an enticement for ever newer and braver ideas. Architecture, however, is that kind of art that no great plans can ever be realised if nobody wishes to build anything. This has been the problem of Helsinki's centre. Whilst the dream of a monumental centre for the capital persists, prominent institutions were first decentralised and then - as

CENTRAL RAILWAY
STATION ,
Eliel Saarinen, 1914

during the last decade - dissolved and privatised in the euphoria of debureaucratisation. However, even in the deepest depths of the depression at the beginning of the 1990s the decision was taken to break the void of the urban core.

In spring 1993 an international architectural competition was arranged for the Museum of Contemporary Art. Out of more than 500 entries, the American Steven Holl's "Chiasma" was thought the best. Its massive sculptured form is now rising behind the equestrian statue of Marshal Mannerheim. Its enclosed form opens only to the south, it seeks no contact with the older buildings, but rises from the urban milieu. A site next to the museum has been allocated for the next new building, the glass cube of the Sanomatalo newspaper office designed by Antti-Matti Siikala and Jan Söderlund. Helsinkians sigh and try to adjust to the idea that even here it is possible to build.

CENTRAL RAILWAY STATION,
MAIN HALL

The housing shortage was managed more effectively in the 1920s. In accordance with Jung's town plan, New Vallila was built as an idyllic stone town in the 1920s as an extension to the earlier Wooden Vallila. Together with Bertel Liljequist, Armas Lindgren designed apartments for Kone ja Silta on Block 555 (bordered by Kangasalantie, Somerontie,

Sammatintie and Anjalantie) which brought a new type of house to the urban complex, the great courtyard block. Begun in 1917, it was not completed until 1929, and even then without the washhouse and kindergarten in the courtyard. This citadel-like building, with its beautifully planted gardens, created a pleasing environment for its numerous tenants. With its symmetrical great courtyard blocks and narrow lamella buildings, New Vallila was the first residential district in which modern housing design plus central and local government financing and loans made it possible for people to live reasonably well in a solidly urban environment.

■ HAKANIEMI

Wooden Käpylä became the idyll of the 1920s. For Birger Brunila and Otto-I. Meurman's town plan, Martti Välikangas designed wooden houses employing element technology in which classical ornamentation and cheerful colours combined to give each house a pleasing individuality within an overall homogeneity. In their deference to the Finnish wooden town heritage, the gardens as well as the siting of the houses, brought a local flavour to an overall plan inspired by international garden city theory.

According to the competition entries of young architects, Etu-Töölö was to have become Finland's first picturesque art nouveau district at the turn of the century. However, due to the vicissitudes of economic life, its construction was postponed for the most part until the end of the 1920s. Bertel Jung ironed out the problems in the 1908 town plan and, as in New Vallila, ensured in his elevation plan that all the architects would conform to the principle of a uniform streetscape. Thus Temppeliaukio grew into an elegant residential district of red-brick, enclosed courtyard buildings with two-room as well as six-room apartment acquiring equally splendid facades. However, as the buildings were owned by private housing companies, they refused to combine their grounds into large, gardened courts as Jung had wished, but fenced in their own properties.

The prestige of Töölö was supplemented by a number of schools and a couple of churches. The final touch was given by Parliament Building. Before J.S. Sirén's granite faced monument was inaugurated in 1931, many competitions had been held and much arm twisting over which of the many desirable city sites would be chosen. The advantage of the Töölö plot was that it permitted a suitably prestigious milieu. However, with increasing traffic, the railway first acquired more land for its marshalling yard, and nobody wished to construct any new buildings in the neighbourhood.

The town plan, however, was redrawn each decade. And with equal futility passionate idealists and competition architects produced their bold new ideas. In the 1950s, Helsinki even tried to find a solution by inviting the country's leading architect, Alvar Aalto, but even his grandiose vision of a terraced plaza, of marble-clad cultural buildings reflected on the waters of the bay and traffic organised along Vapaudenkatu (Freedom Street) never progressed further than drawings and scale models.

In 1936, and again in 1956, J.S. Sirén proposed plans to bring at least the nearby area into harmony with Parliament Building, but even these were ignored. Bronze statues of past presidents were brought to guard the palace on Arkadianmäki hill, but the road in front gobbled up so much of lawn that passing buses almost tickle P.E. Svinhufvud's toes. Mannerheimintie remains one of the city's most vital thoroughfares and, together with the railway, it cleaves Helsinki into awkward sectors in a north-south direction.

Mannerheimintie, the main car route through Töölö to the north, is continuously becoming more congested however many efforts have been made over the decades to divert traffic elsewhere. Sometimes on a quiet Sunday you are astonished to realise how very urban and continental is the architecture of the sturdy residential blocks lining the road between the old Exhibition Centre and the former Tullinpuomi tollgate. In the

■ WOODEN VALLILA

1920s, architects played with symmetrical facade compositions and elegant classical decorative motifs. Just before the war, the as yet unbuilt parts of Töölö were opened in accordance with the tenets of functionalism. In the final years of the 1930s, designers concentrated on improving plan solutions for apartments and only compromised their strict asceticism in respect to the stair halls. Beyond the grey facades you can see glimpses of red or green walls and ceilings, shining in competition to the chromed grills of the newfangled lifts. The deciduous trees in the skimpy gardens are already thick in foliage and beautifully soften the streetscape.

On Topeliuksenkatu, running parallel to the west of Mannerheimintie, attention was paid to that important novelty of 1930s' modernism; the balcony. Thanks to the park beneath Töölö Church, the scene is airy and light. It is best described by Helvi Hämäläinen in her novel *Säädyllinen murhenäytelmä* (A respectable tragedy) from 1941: "The new Helsinki, which has grown much larger than the older districts of

Kaivopuisto, Katajanokka, Eira and Kruununhaka, makes its houses smooth like boxes, with things like bathtubs fixed to the walls: each family has its own balcony, or pushes part of the room out of the window so it's like a porch. It paints its houses pale yellow, pale green and silver grey, and in order to capture more sunlight, mixes chips of green bottle glass with the plaster - an invention by which the inventive architect manages to get whole rows of houses to glisten in the same way. The passerby screws up his eyes and goes to have a closer look to see whether the chips are really glass, as they seem to be. The stair halls are fantastic, the walls bright blue like irises or flaming red, yellow or green. Each one tries to think up something more surprising: many of the walls have reliefs, giant gilded circles which give the hall a sense of good taste and luxury, or widen it so it suddenly opens into a hall with a fountain in the middle, and for those who can't think up anything else, put up an incredibly huge mirror. The lifts, which operate in the nickel and glass well, are rosewood, mahogany or walnut lined boxes, too small, and in their red glowing interior you feel awfully cramped. In those houses, where they have tried for simplicity, the lifts have been lined with fair Finnish birch. The New Helsinki also plays with its hilarious inventions inside the flats; it builds in them tiny cupboards which it calls kitchens, with glass doors or simple wrought-iron gates to separate them from the other rooms; it builds in them windowless halls that get their light from the other rooms, and equips them with fireplaces in the English style, from black marble or granite, fireplaces that more often remind you of gravestones and in which the Finn almost never lights a fire."

After the war, when the best residential areas were considered the suburbs, the massive blocks of Etu and Taka Töölö were condemned as "barracks". The same criticism was levelled at the tall apartment blocks set obliquely to the road between the end of Mannerheimintie and Central Park. They were always viewed from the road, never from the verdant park end. Nowadays this smart row of high houses attracts only admiration for the excellent and intelligent way the postwar housing shortage was solved.

At the same time, the blocks of three-storey homes built further to the west in Meilahti, have enjoyed unreserved acceptance from the beginning. In summer, the profusion of trees and bushes almost completely conceal these otherwise characterless buildings, and the proximity of the sea and the charm of old villas of Meilahti are additional magical attractions.

Where Paciuksenkatu becomes Puistotie at Munkkiniemi, you arrive in that part of the city for ever associated with the name of Eliel Saarinen. According to his Munkkiniemi-Haaga Plan from 1915, the lands then owned by the Stenius company were to be build on so they have graduated from a low density area detached and terraced houses by the shore to a high density metropolis of massive enclosed blocks lining the main thoroughfares. Saarinen's organic grasp can best be appreciated from the scale model in the City Museum. All that can be recognised on the actual site are the alignments of the main roads, the small row house on Hollantilaisentie and the Casino, subsequently the Military Academy and now the Public Management Centre.

Most of Munkkiniemi was built in two stages, before and soon after the war. With the exception of a few villas, Munkkivuori and North and South Haaga to the north remained for the postwar years. The terrain contoured town plans for South Haaga and Munkkivuori have offered sheltered playgrounds places for two generations already. Now the population of the old suburbs is ageing, and the schools, where there were two teaching shifts in the 1950s, are emptying. Young families move to the next ring of suburbs, to Espoo and Vantaa - unless they manage to get a place in one of the more central newer suburbs like Ruoholahti or Little Huopalahti.

When the train leaves the Central Railway Station for the north, you can admire the expressiveness of central Helsinki. The sparkling white of Alvar Aalto's Finlandia Hall from the 1970s alone on the banks of Töölö Bay. Fresh grass struggles for supremacy in the

■

CITY THEATRE ,
Timo Penttilä, 1972

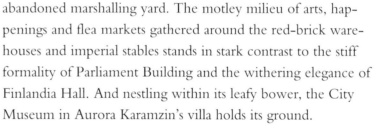

FINNISH NATIONAL OPERAHOUSE,
Eero Hyvämäki,
Jukka Karhunen,
Risto Parkkinen, 1992

abandoned marshalling yard. The motley milieu of arts, happenings and flea markets gathered around the red-brick warehouses and imperial stables stands in stark contrast to the stiff formality of Parliament Building and the withering elegance of Finlandia Hall. And nestling within its leafy bower, the City Museum in Aurora Karamzin's villa holds its ground.

Since 1992 the new Opera House has closed the northwestern corner of Töölö Bay. Designed by Eero Hyvämäki, Jukka Karhunen and Risto Parkkinen, this cultural edifice shows its best side to the bay. The Mannerheimintie and Helsinginkatu corner is cramped, albeit Kain Tapper's sculpture tries to win space from the traffic roaring past.

The gaunt buildings of Siltasaari appear as intrepid fortresses on the far side of Eläintarha Bay, varying delightfully in expression with the weather and light. The City Theatre by Timo Penttilä, rests rhythmically on the green slope of Eläintarha Park. The villas standing precariously above the gorge make you pray that no further encroachment upon their living space will be made by yet another railway track. The renovated Olympic Stadium, young Finland's icon of a national identity based on sport, has regained its shining whiteness. At Linnanmäki

83

Amusement Park, you are reminded that this is a must for every child in summer, and shame on you if you don't find the time.

From the window you cannot see deep into the two worlds of Pasila. There is in fact little difference between them, the administrative buildings to the east are only slightly more depressing and the western side is lightened by Ilmo Valjakka's joyfully detached architecture of the Magazine and Radio buildings. Should these be called post-modernist?

■

LITTLE HUOPALAHTI

The new suburb of Little Huopalahti from the 1990s is largely the work of Matti Visanti and Reijo Jallinoja, and makes earlier architectural distractions look very tame. This distinctive area is a protest against the right angle. The streets curve, the buildings vary in size and shape, and their facades are full of colour and ornament. The jewel in the crown is Jallinoja's massive terraced house, the pyramid shape of which pops up surprisingly from many parts of the city. Little Huopalahti entices you to walk. Some people are happy with all the surprises, others become nervous. At long last something new! But why always something new?

A REAL CITY

The heart of Helsinki is, according to all observations and definitions, severe but handsome. Cobbled squares, streets and multistorey buildings within a grid plan, Bulevardi and Esplanade, a respectable number of church towers and still the odd factory chimney - everything in fact that belongs to a real European city.

In configuration, the Helsinki of the Vironniemi headland is geographically and architectonically strikingly clear, both horizontally and vertically. Waves from the Gulf of Finland wash against the embanked waterfront and the city's silhouette has been spared the vulgarity of ever higher skyscrapers. The sea is never too far from anywhere, and Central Park brings the lush verdancy of the surrounding countryside into its heart.

During the last hundred years, on the ancient arable fields betwixt the sea and the forests around Helsinki, a miscellany of villas, suburbs, neighbourhoods and industrial zones have been built. Over the last fifty years the size and style of residential areas has fluctuated violently with the vicissitudes of economic conditions, social customs, planning principles and the whims of fashion. An increasingly efficient road and rail network now binds the different fragments of the city, the suburbs built either sparsely or densely, high or low, gradually or in one go, in colour or in black-and-white. Now Helsinki has so many different types of areas, that with good luck quite dissimilar people can find the milieu of their dreams. This, too, is part of a real city.

The world's shortest metro takes you in twenty minutes from the recently completed Ruoholahti in the west to Mellunmäki in the east. The new district centre under construction at Vuosaari will soon divide the metro into two branches at Itäkeskus. If the new harbour is built, then, with the closing of the old shipyard, the roar of lorries will become Vuosaari's headache. Transportwise, a headland is always an awkward place. To the north the railway has triumphed over the roads in its competition for the people's hearts. To the west, the lavishly widened highway feeds a continuous stream of cars owned by former Helsinkians who have fled to Espoo and Kirkkonummi. In the centre nothing can compare to the traditional comfort of trams, and the importance of pedestrians and cyclists has at long last been recognised. After all, it's not always winter in Helsinki.

All Finnish roads eventually lead to Helsinki. The centre is where everything important happens, even if palaces of culture have been built in the district centres of Itäkeskus, Malmi and Kannelmäki, and churches, schools, libraries, colleges and other facilities offer a busy programme for suburbanites.

■ MÄNTYNIEMI
PRESIDENTIAL RESIDENCE
Reima and Raili Pietilä,
1992

Helsinki is like an onion, and everyone fancies is juicy centre. Senate Square is Finland's main stage, and Esplanade, Aleksanterinkatu and Mannerheimintie its parade grounds. Processions and demonstrations, physical and spiritual culture, witness their importance. When the provinces present themselves in summer, they take over Senate Square, and create their carnival fearless of the contrasts of the architecture, moods and imaginations of the classical setting of the former grand duchy. ●

Shopping in
Kallio

Mummy works in Irja Markkanen's shop.

It's called a Colonial Store.

I pop in there on the way home from the kintergarden.

Pirkko Saisio Mummy grinds Oka coffee in the coffee mill. She puts cardboard pictures of cars on top to keep the packets stiff.

After Irja Markkanen goes out for lunch, mummy asks the elderly customers whether they want the car pictures in their coffee packets.

In the evening we paste all the cards mummy's got in the Oka coffee album.

In spring, when the album's full and we've posted it to the Oka Coffee Company's office, I get an Oka Coffee car.

It's got a chrome steering wheel and chromed wheel spokes. Even so the bigger boys don't take from me it to play flick cars with in the park, because flick cars are much lighter, they're from plastic.

The following evening mother brings home a box of Buffalo Bill chewing gum. I think I'll start collecting Buffalo Bill labels now.   >

Uncle Turto sells us milk on the sly. There's a milk strike on.

Mummy's hidden the milk jug in her leather shopping bag.

Once the shop's empty, Uncle Turto takes the jug and fills it with a deft flip of the wrist.

"After all, the kids have got to have it," says Uncle Turto. At home I drink three glasses straight off. It leaves me with a milk moustache.

"Uncle Turto's got pals in the dairy," says mummy.

★

I don't believe in Father Christmas any more. That's why I get pocket money so I can buy presents on his behalf.

I'll buy a clothes brush for mummy. It's from pink leather and there's a zipper so you can open the back. Inside there's a needle and pink thread.

And there's money left for the others: flints for dad's lighter; a quarter-kilo of coffee from Elanto for granny; a shaving brush for grandpa and two hankies for Aunty Ulla, one green and one checked for ordinary use.

But mummy's present is the best. So I hope they all notice it.

★

Once we've phoned Sorsakivi the butcher and the Hirvikallios (Sorsakivi said, Shoot it! and Hirvikallio said, Shoot it dead!), we started to get a bit cheesed off, especially when Sorsakivi the butcher has started answering the phone with a stupid 'Hallo' or just 'Sorsakivi'.

We set off for the stationers. It's run by two old ladies, they must be at least forty. We're in the second year at grammar school and we've been learning English for a term now.

Real cool like we ask, in English naturally: "Have you a pair of scissors?"

The oldies don't understand and neither do we understand their sign language and stupid mutterings.

"They're from abroad," whispers one of the oldies. Outside its sleeting. You really do pity people who've absolutely no international experience.

★

I've eaten them all: sour black bread, yeast bread, white split loaf and French breads like baguette, croissants and cheese horns, breads flavoured with carrots, linseed, cumin, malt, syrup, blood and olives, black Russian bread, mom's bread rolls, popadums, naans, rice cakes and cruscas, chapatis naturally, Väinämöinen's coat buttons, Big Sisters and Little Brothers, Travellers and Niskavuori baps, oatmeal cakes and rye wholemeal, wedding loaves and Yule sötsurs, unleavened bread and barley yeast bread. There's an ad in Tipi's window in Vaasankatu for dried bread.

I buy three kilos of it.

It's packed in a thick brown paper. The last time I saw paper like this was at the exhibition of Japanese packing art in Stockholm or the programme of the Helsinki City Theatre.

I thought to myself, is Dried Bread something flavoured with blueberries, aniseed, fennel, chamomile or stitch-wort. Or is it some kind of ersatz bread from tree bark.

It's not.

It's just stale, unsold black bread, put aside to dry. And I've got three kilos of it.

★

In the Sakarinkatu secondhand bookshop I look in vain for a van Gulik detective story about the 7th century Chinese Judge Dee which I haven't read, and, surprisingly, come across a collection of Chekhov's short stories printed in Petroskoi in the early Fifties which smells like good books often do: old printer's ink. My problem is this: do I pay for it with one of the thousand mark notes I've just withdrawn from the bank to pay the garage for fitting gaskets to something in my Lada. I offer the shopkeeper one of them: "You don't expect me to change that? You must be dreaming," he says. Next to me, browsing through a pile of Batman and Superman comics, is a bent old gent in an overcoat that looks like it came out of Gogol's St. Petersburg. "I don't suppose you could change this?" I ask jokingly. "Sure," he says straightaway, and pulls out a thick wad of thousand-mark notes from his breast pocket. "Which one would you like to change it for?" ●

■ NORTH MAKASIININKATU

■ OLD MARKET HALL

94

■ BULEVARDI

■ HÄMEENTIE

■ TEHTAANKATU

95

■ ARKADIANKATU

■ SATAMAKATU

■

UUDENMAANKATU

96

■ PENGERKATU

■

BULEVARDI

■ ISO-ROOBERTINKATU

97

Antti Raivio

Tales from

Etu-Töölö

The first thing I remember about Töölö is the neon lights of the Ritz cinema. Fantastic, I thought, just like Walt Disney's name on the cover of Mickey Mouse. We were going to see The Jungle Book. Father, mother, my brother and I. I was wearing the Snoopy shirt mum made, my brother was sucking sweets, mum looked longingly at the studio flats on the top floor of the Lallukka

artists' home and, whilst the rest of us were at the cinema, dad popped into the Elite restaurant. First glancing at the menu. It must have been spring, because you could smell the grass. It was a great day, because I had a banana milk shake afterwards at the HM café. The buildings looked dull compared to my milk shake. Mother explained that this is Töölö. "Daft name. Sounds like you're being sick," says my brother. We fetched dad from the pub. Fortunately, we'd come by train.

During my first year at the University of Dramatic Art I dossed down in Apollo school as I'd no money to travel back and forth between Hyrylä and Helsinki. Töölö seemed to be incredibly quiet. Did anyone actually live there? In the evenings most of the windows remained in darkness. Maybe they were all hot on saving electricity? I'd just see a few old grannies when I went for my morning run. Every other day, every other house flew the Finnish flag at half mast. In no capital city, not this close to the centre, could it be so quiet! It seemed that the Freud, Engels, Mark & Jung Group's piece was dead right for Töölö: "I've heard there's a place over there, were grannies can be proud to die..."

It hadn't occurred to me then that this place was undergoing a managed structural change.

It's difficult to describe Töölö. Most people pass it by travelling down Mannerheimintie, Runeberginkatu or Mechelininkatu. The most they do is get themselves patched up at the Töölö accident centre. They don't understand that Töölö's a fortress, surrounded by a wall of public buildings to protect it from what it doesn't want. Parliament Building, National Museum, Finlandia Hall, Töölönlahti bay, Opera House, the old Fair Centre, Sibelius Academy, Helsinki Art Hall, Natural History Museum, Temppeliaukio Church, Swedish School of Economics and Business Administration, Helsinki School of Economics and Business Administration, Hietaniemi Cemetery, Guards' Battalion barracks and Hesperia Hospital form a circle enclosing a world to which you must learn to adjust.

My mate Essi once tried to set up a hot-dog stall in the park next to the Elanto shop, the same place where there's now a big statue to the singer and songwriter Georg 'Jori' Malmsten. His nosh was the best in Finland - well, after Jaska's Grill, that is - but because the residents thought the stall caused a disturbance and wasn't painted in the traditional virgin white but was covered in graffiti, letters to the editor soon started to pour in. And bingo! Would you kindly move two blocks down towards Kamppi!

When the Q Theatre group was looking for premises, we came across the old Astra cinema in Tunturikatu, which was so well concealed in the middle of Töölö that nobody knew anything about it - except the old locals of course. A small group of furtive-looking Uurim-Pentecostalist fanatics had camped out at the Astra. All that remained of them was an altar cross made from loo tiles, a half-finished font dug in the floor and a chamber pot belonging to one of the younger members of the congregation. This we rented - the cinema that is - and it became my home. The largest bachelor pad in Finland! At first I dossed down in the theatre buffet, then for about a year in the projectionist's room which the actor Mikko Reitala had furnished. It felt that we were the only thing happening in Töölö. Even the market hall next door went bust and the Uurim gang split into Uurims and Buurims.

Nowadays, you don't often see flags flying at half mast. Passers-by are more likely to be happy couples pushing prams. Whereas Sörnäinen became full of pubs, here it's still possible to make a living selling bread and buns. And where the always-just-as-cheap Rabatti and Alepa supermarkets pushed their way in elsewhere, stores the size of living rooms still survive in Töölö. Here you don't only think about what to buy, but who to buy it from. The locals hate buses, but dig trams. Maybe one day they'll get round to loading buses with the chunks of abstract statuary they loathe so much, where you can't distinguish Mika Waltari from an ex-president. And perhaps replace them with a gigantic statue to the actor Tauno Palo on a tram.

"Are you heavy-footed?" asked this old-woman's voice when I was moving into Apollonkatu from Töölönkatu. I turned round. The upstairs neighbour had appeared at the open front door to inspect the new residents. "The former occupants were. This is a very decent and quiet house," she said and went on her way. I could detect an element of reproach when she spotted the cigarettes on the table. The apartment upstairs, next to her flat, had been rented out to the Helsinki University's Faculty of Seismology. Nobody ever goes there. Obviously there's nothing to measure. There aren't any tottering buildings in Töölö.

The structural change advances slowly. When the next people move in, the former newcomers will already have become part of the scenery. In the evenings the local lads and lassies head for the centre because nothing world-shattering ever happens here. Other than those who disappear into the Bermuda Triangle - the Elite, Kuu Kuu and Botta pubs.

Töölö by night is beautiful. It smells of silence. With just a suggestion of garlic wafting in from Jaska's Grill. It's beautiful. As even the newspaper boy can confirm. ●

■ HELSINKI CITY TRAM DRIVERS

From the blue

When sharpness softens. When contours fade. When nothing prevents you seeing the impenetrable darkness over there and over here, as all borders fuse – no sky, no sea, no horizon. Just blue.

To become one with the invisibility growing outside the window, the tones of Finlandia Hall fall silent, the far shore of Töölö Bay vanishes. Only the blue. The big blue.

Blue is longing, mystique and myths. It is nostalgia and faraway dreams, the lure of death – walk and walk o'er the ice, who knows where it ends, towards the deep rumble on the far side of the distant vastness, the snow crunches, the cold numbs, there's no return, land and sanctuary are lost for ever, just walk and walk in the ever deepening blue.

Märta Tikkanen

There's also that kind of longing, Luc Besson captured it in The Big Blue, which lures stalwart young men, draws them on, ever further, ever deeper, until all's too late. Nothing any more, just when fulfillment and completion, victory over the known and the unknown, over dreaded presentiment, is within reach. Then.

All is over.

This wistfulness of Northern man, light that elates us so we float above the ground at midsummer and in ecstasy, compensating the darkness we must endure, suffer from year to year, awaiting the brief highlights of our existence: all this waiting, to much to bear. Because it is so long, because the darkness is so impenetrable, so inescapable, just for this reason we love the blue moment. Cling to it. Sink into it.

Sink. Vanish. Disintegrate and capitulate. Just so.

But also, and perhaps just as much: the opposite.

A blue moment without demands. Nobody sees, knows, we vanish into infinity, without trace, without guilt. We rest in nothingness.

Only the essentials. To breath. To rest. To be.

To wake again. Perhaps.

And to know, that all the time beneath the ice, the crust, and the stone lies concealed a heat, a fire that burns more fiercely the thicker the glacier, ice and fire, the white glow, blue flame deep down under.

To be left untouched, unseen, unfelt. Just know: this is the moment when power concentrates and becomes materia, this is the fuel for the time of night and darkness, a time we must endure and experience, in order that sometime, at last, possibly

yes, certainly

we can blast the way open and live. Danger transformed, converted into a power that carries forward and which will become knowledge and action, presence and charging and energy, a return from dreams and tranquility, disintegrated to become one again, to grow, be hurled into time, the greatest and simplest of miracles:

tomorrow.

To grow out of the blue. Like Helsinki from the sea. ●

■ WINTER SWIMMERS

■ HELSINKI SWIMMING STADIUM
Jorma Järvi, 1938

▲   ESPLANADE PARK

■   HAKANIEMI MARKET SQUARE

113

■ ALEKSANTERINKATU AT CHRISTMAS

ROWING STADIUM, HUMALLAHTI

■ CELEBRATING HELSINKI DAY AT
HIETALAHTI MARKET SQUARE

Feelings

Probably every Helsinkian has a personal attachment to some church, shop or café, or certain stallholder in one of the open markets, its colourful mood or ambience when empty. Many prefer one theatre more than another. Some enjoy the atmosphere of a first night or a major concert by the Helsinki Philharmonic Orchestra or Radio Symphony Orchestra, even though nobody bothers to dress up for the occasion any more. Others again prefer to enjoy theatre or music on their own or with a friend. When news comes of the international successes of the City Theatre Dance Group or the Helsinki Junior Strings - that child of long-term resident Hungarians Géza and Csaba Szilvay - there's jubilation among the wide circle of the friends of modern dance and young classical music performers. Studying at one of the Adult Education Centres means spiritual food for tens of thousands of city dwellers. The main building of the Finnish Adult Education Centre throbs with the optimism of classic civilisation. Above the main entrance is Gunnar Finne's relief of a man walking in the clouds, and in the lobby is Sam Vanni's Contrapunctus. Opposite the school is the Brahis recreation ground. Probably nowhere else have so many generations skated and played football.

STATUE OF A WORKING-CLASS MOTHER , Panu Patomäki, 1996

Many cherished places have disappeared. Of Helsinki's fifty cinemas in the 1950s, most are now but fond memories, as too are nearly all of the public saunas. Helsinkians feel impoverished when for economic reasons or the whims of fashion, a familiar shop, branch bank, café or restaurant disappears. Forgetful of his own contrariety he praises the cosy corner store but shops at the hypermarket because of its wide assortment, special offers and convenient parking. Occasionally market forces even work in

■ HELSINKI FESTIVAL: HELSINKI CITY ORCHESTRA CONCERT IN ST. JOHN'S CHURCH (above) AND A THEATRICAL PERFORMANCE IN VANHAKIRKKO PARK (below).

■ TEMPPELIAUKIO CHURCH
■ MIKONKATU

the interests of some special site. For example, the Wärtsilä Group, which once coveted the site of the Tennis Palace for its head office, no longer exists, but this personable building survives converted into a museum and a cinema. The culturally historic Kämp is being returned from a bank into a hotel following the bank's demise in a merger.

Mostly beloved places are protected by the feelings of the townsfolk. There was a scheme for building over the Josafatinkallio rock park off Helsinginkatu. In spite of its stone heart this was an oasis in an otherwise densely built area. The group that brought the project to a standstill probably feel they have given the rocks a new lease of life. The laying of essential additional tracks threatened the decorative villas of Linnunlaulu. Opposition from the friends of history and the milieu forced the railway engineers to come up with another solution. Defenders of Old Town Bay, a nature conservation area unique in a metropolis, managed to persuade the city to build the nearby Viiki Science Park and housing estate with due consideration. The Vuosaari harbour project, the purpose of which is to release the city's existing harbour areas for residential building, has been battled over for years. At least the most sensitive nature sites must be protected. Differences in outlook appear in even the smallest places: supporters of juvenile and teenage footballers erected an ugly inflatable hall in Hesperia Park, which to others meant an essential part of urban park culture. There is much for Helsinkians to ponder over when thinking of ways to appreciate and cherish the urban nature. ●

■ TEATTERI JURKKA
■ GROUP THEATRE

Aarne Laurila

■   HELSINKI FESTIVAL MARQUEE

Immigrants in Helsinki

KULDEP SINGH, AMARJEET
KAUR, PRITHI SANDHU *and*
RAKEESH *and* PINKI BHATIA, India

"Finland's a good country, but the
people are more reserved than in
India, and friends are also difficult to
make."

SUSANNA SFARADI, Israel

"Life would be more beautiful in
Finland if there was more sun."

■

WANG FENG MING,
China

"I teach Tai Ji Quan and
Qi Gong at Helsinki
University. I love my
work. Tai Ji spreads
friendship and through
cooperation we achieve
better results."

■

ATSUKO OKUDA and
KIIKO UZAWA, Japan

"Many people say in
Finland that Finns and
Japanese have much in
common. We have
lived many years in
Finland and don't think
this is so. Finns are
Finns, and Japanese are
Japanese. Nationality
has long traditions."

GRZEGORZ
KOSIERADZKI,
Poland

"I'm bilingual. Polish
is my mother
tongue. I spend my
days teaching Finnish
in a Finnish Upper
Secondary School for
adults. Bilingualism
means two different
ways of expressing
yourself. Bicultura-
lism allows two ways
of viewing the
surrounding world.
It is a bridge to
multiculturalism and
universal culture.
Poland has given me
wonderful, strong,
living and nourishing
roots. Finland is my
window to the
world."

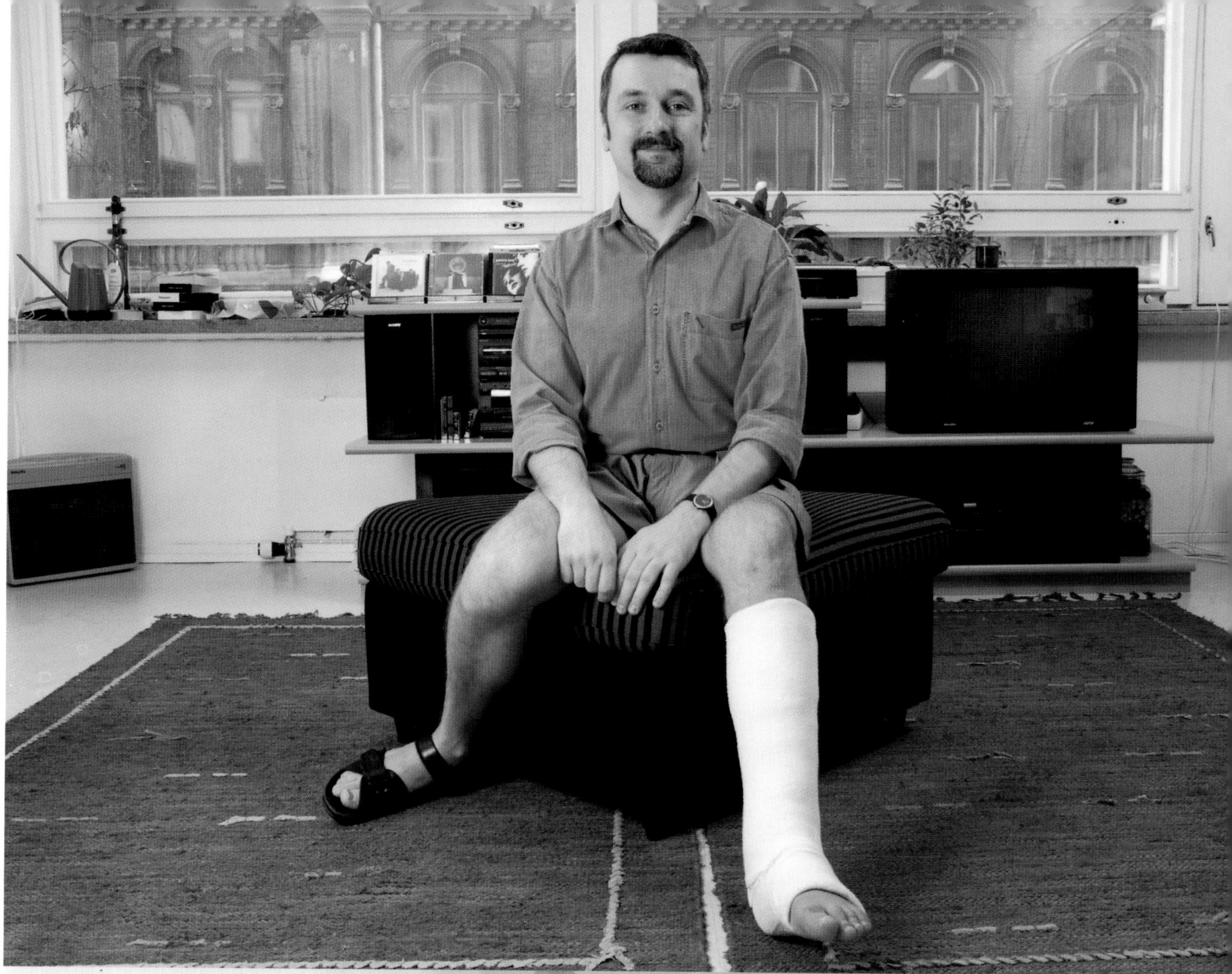

JANET PENA JESSICA,
JENNIFER and VANES-
SA TALLEDO;
PATRICIA, SANDRA and
GINA TALLEDO-
FRÖJDMAN;
YNGRID and CHARLOT-
TA TALLEDO, Peru

"Finns are honest,
but it's too quiet
here."

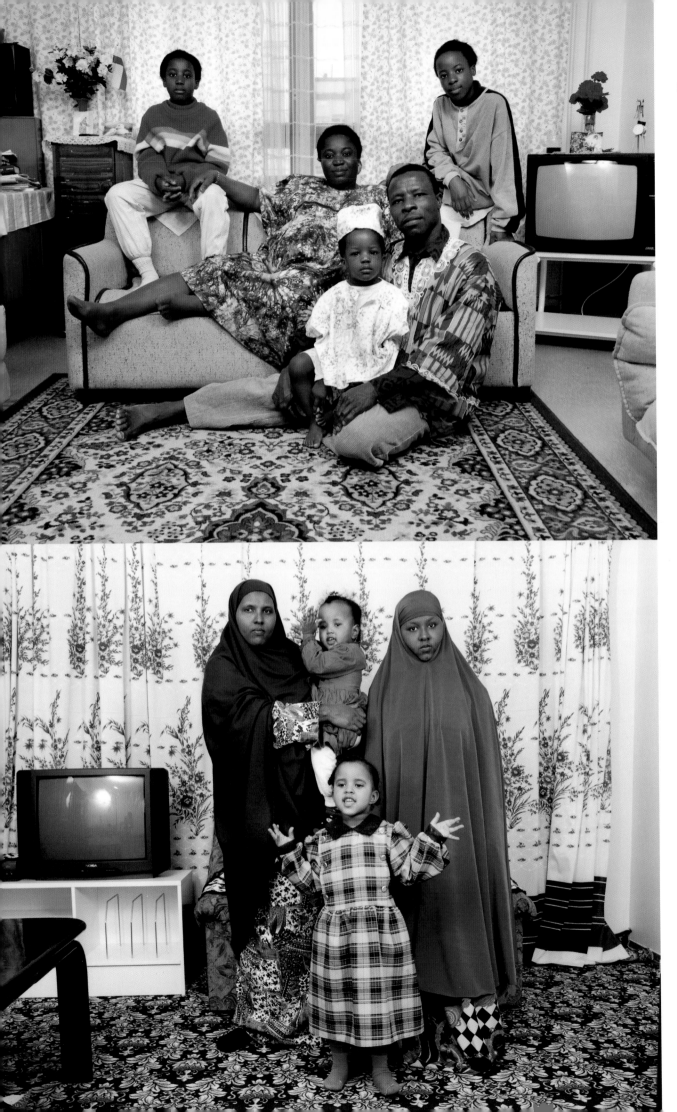

OLUCHI,
URSULA-MARY,
NNAEMEKA,
STEPHEN and
UGONNA
ANYAMELE,
Nigeria

"A home far from home."

THE MAHAMUD
JAMA DAAR FAMILY:
FOWSIA ALI YUSUF,
HAMDI MAHAMUD
JAMA, SOFIA
MAHAMUD JAMA,
HALIMO MAHAMUD
JAMA, Somalia

"It's good living in
Finland, but there are
two things which
irritate us. Firstly, the
weather is very different from Somalia, and
secondly, the Finnish
people are very reserved and it's difficult
making contact with
them. Without these
two annoying things it
would be easier to live
in Finland."

ÖZEN ERDING and JESSICA KELLGREN, Sweden

"Our profession brought us to the Finnish National Ballet. Helsinki is a peaceful and safe place to live in. What's beautiful about the city is its Russian architecture and that it is surrounded by the sea and forests."

JUHO, LIDIJA, OLGA, ANNA and ARTUR ORKOLAINEN and EVGENI and JULIA BELOF, Russia/Ingermanland

"We are happy to have come to Finland. Many things are better here than in Russia. Our children are at work and the little ones are at school. For old people and children, life's good in Finland."

SEA CANOEISTS

133

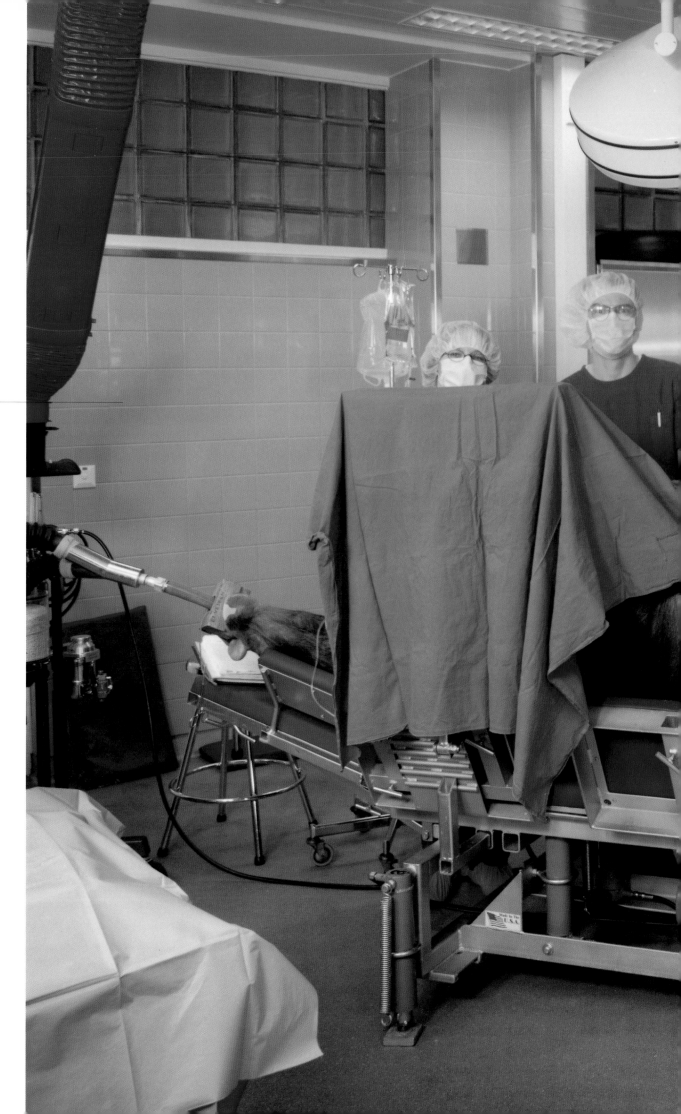

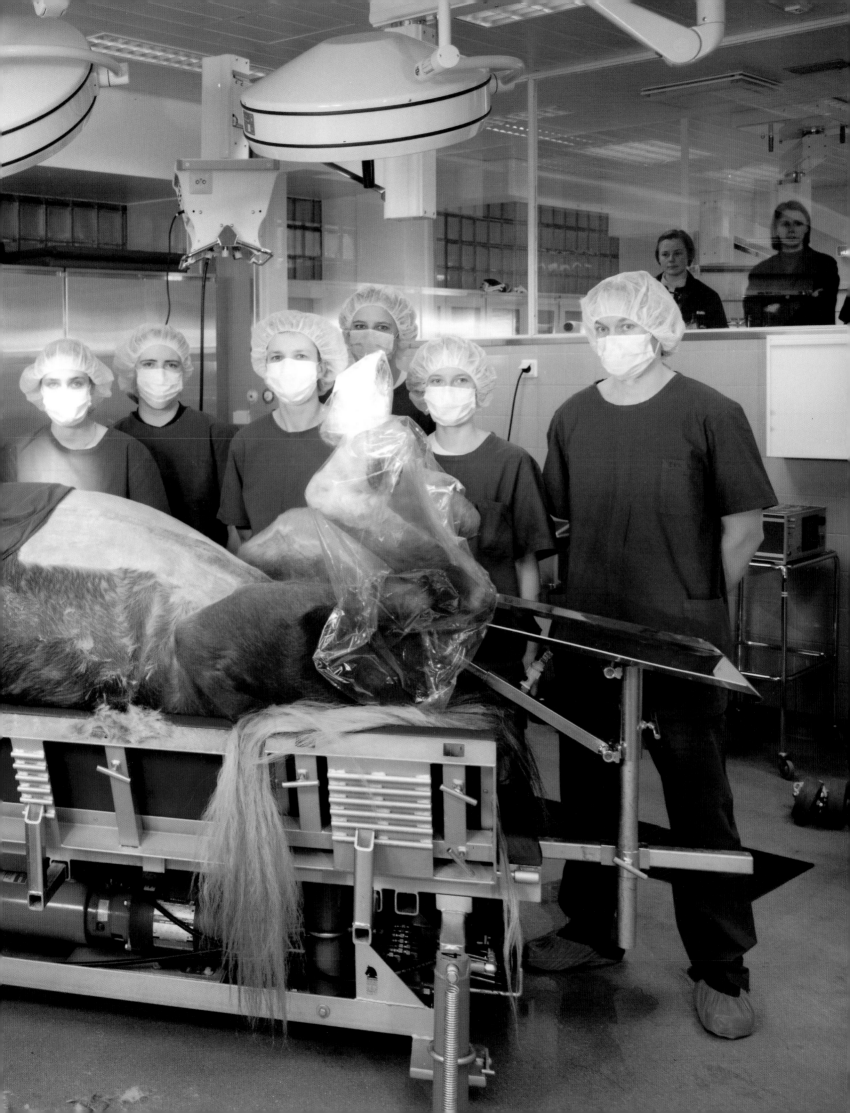

A dreamy dream

Here's that guy again. Time after time, even if others come more often. But this one's so odd: he comes up to the bar, sits down, has a beer, sometimes a whisky, and never says a word. Hours on end. Well, he talks in a way like, to himself - no sound emerges, but his expression changes, like he's listening to something new. Or perhaps he's just pretending.

I mean, I've nothing against that, others shout like urban apes after they've had a couple. Now he's on a pint of Three Lager and I bet you a hundred marks he won't say a word.

Harri Ruohomäki

"Thanks, keep the change. You know,
I've been having this odd dream. D'you mind if I tell you about it?"

Now what's happening. He talks. And we've been looking at each other over the bar for at least three years.

"Yea. Why not. Fire away."

"Well, it always starts like this: it's late afternoon, in spring, I'm in my flat, where I can see the living room and the kitchen. It's on the first floor of an old renovated

136

wooden house, the work's not finished yet, the glazed double doors to the living room are still unpainted. The flat's furnished with old furniture, there's a huge Billnäs desk in the living room, a thick green carpet, a tall palm and an old black piano.

There's a 13 year-old, fair-haired, skinny lad with glasses playing the piano. He's not playing very well, but quite fluently: We're all heroes, when you look closely ... The boy has a sad look on his face, he doesn't smile, just stares at the piano.

Then this woman bangs a mug of tea down on the kitchen table, slopping tea over the old unpainted top, the playing stops. She starts to yell, 'For Christ's sake, first you phone and say you'll be late and then when you do come, you say you can't take the lad even though we agreed. It's just the same as when we were still married. You can damn well go back to that bitch of yours. D'you hear, GO!'

The woman is dark-haired, 35 years old, beautiful, wearing a jersey. The man's got a beard and long hair, and stares down at the table top. Then, after a moment and without saying a word, he walks to the hallway and leaves. The woman nervously grabs the tea mug and takes a slurp. The boy comes into the kitchen, sits on a chair by the window and looks out apathetically. Both are silent for a while, the taps drips in the sink, outside a car starts up noisily.

Then the boy starts to talk quietly, 'Aija, can't I meet my real father one day?'

The woman rests her head in her hands, elbows on the table. Then she answers, 'I don't know. Samppa, go and see whether Tuukka's in the yard.'

Samppa looks at the woman, the woman at the table, then he takes his glasses off, pushes his hair back to the left, gets up and walks quietly out of the kitchen.

Excuse me, you seem to have other customers. Serve them first. And I'll have another, too. Then perhaps I could continue ..."

Now the guy's really letting go, I wonder if he's popped a pill. I don't care, I'll give him another drink.

"Right. Here we are, carry on."

"Well, then the dream changes to a summer's morning in Helsinki's Railway Square. There's a bus parked in front of the National Theatre and boy scouts are getting out. And this Aija woman comes running up with a cigarette in her fingers, sun glasses pushed up on her brow. And yells from far off, 'Samppa! Samppa, come here! Isn't it great, Tuukka and I have come to meet you.'

Samppa stands quite still, arms hanging down limply, peers at Aija through his glasses, the sun burning his hair, then he pushes his hair back to the left and says quietly, 'Yes, it's great.'

Then Aija takes Samppa's bag, Samppa carries his rucksack and sleeping bag, and they walk to the tramstop talking, 'Guess where you and Tuukka are going next week? Your grand parent's place in the north. And guess what else, Grandpa's bought me a trip to the south because he thinks I haven't been anywhere for ages - and also because we had such a rotten winter.'

Samppa doesn't reply, just stares ahead, mother and sons continue walking.

Then suddenly it's an autumn evening in my dream and I'm again in the flat. The boy Samppa's lying on the living room floor reading, his brother Tuukka's playing with a doll on the same carpet when Aija comes clattering in laden down with shopping bags. The boys glance up but carry on doing what they're doing. But the woman starts talking straight away, 'Hei there! Samppa, guess who phoned me at work today?'

The bigger boy, Samppa, puts down his book, turns to look at Aija, takes his glasses off, pushes his hair back to the left, a look of expectation on his face. And the woman says, 'Kari, your father.'

And then Samppa is left staring, glasses in his hand, sitting on the floor, mouth open but his expression still dubious. Aija pulls her boots off and hangs up her coat, but doesn't look at Samppa, 'Yea, he asked whether he could meet you. I told him you've often asked me about him, but I didn't know where on earth he was living. It's only in Espoo.'

Then my dream moves on to late autumn. Samppa stares out of the window, dog walkers carrying heavy shopping bags cross the road. Raindrops break-up the light on the window pane. A car stops by the roadside, a man gets out and walks with firm steps into a nearby shop. Samppo pushes his glasses up and smooths his hair back. A taxi comes from the left and stops outside the house. A tall slender man with glasses gets out from the back, staggers slightly as he steps into the road. Then looks up at the first-floor window, removes his glasses, pushes back his hair, drops his look to the road, presses his palms to his eyes, and gets back into the taxi. The taxi's rear lights shine on the rain-spattered window.

Inside the flat Samppa takes off his glasses, carelessly pushes back his hair out of habit, goes to the piano and starts to play: We're all heroes ...

Perhaps I'll have another pint still. Thanks, it was a very real experience." ●

- Shall I put the headphones handy?

- I took the guy from the hospital on holiday with me. We popped into this place for a beer, but I never told him it was a gay bar. When the time came to visit the toilet, he needed help with his flies. At least in a place like that they don't stare.

- I had skin grafted from my thighs to my hand. I had to stay inside as my jeans were so tight it hurt to put them on.

- Sometimes in the pub I drink somebody else's beer as it's difficult judging distances with only one eye. My mates just look the other way.

Portraits

of patients

- They phoned me in Helsinki from the north to ask whether it was necessary to amputate. I said, if there's any feeling at all, then send the boy here. There was, in the little finger. We operated on the hand and now it's quite okay.

- Deary me, I should never have agreed to be photographed. Now it's too late.

- These are magic beads, you know. Once I heard someone calling my name, so I turned round, and during that time the beads appeared on my neck. I still don't know who put them there.

- I heard you bust your camera photographing these old darlings.

- I look so really old (in this picture), just like I should.

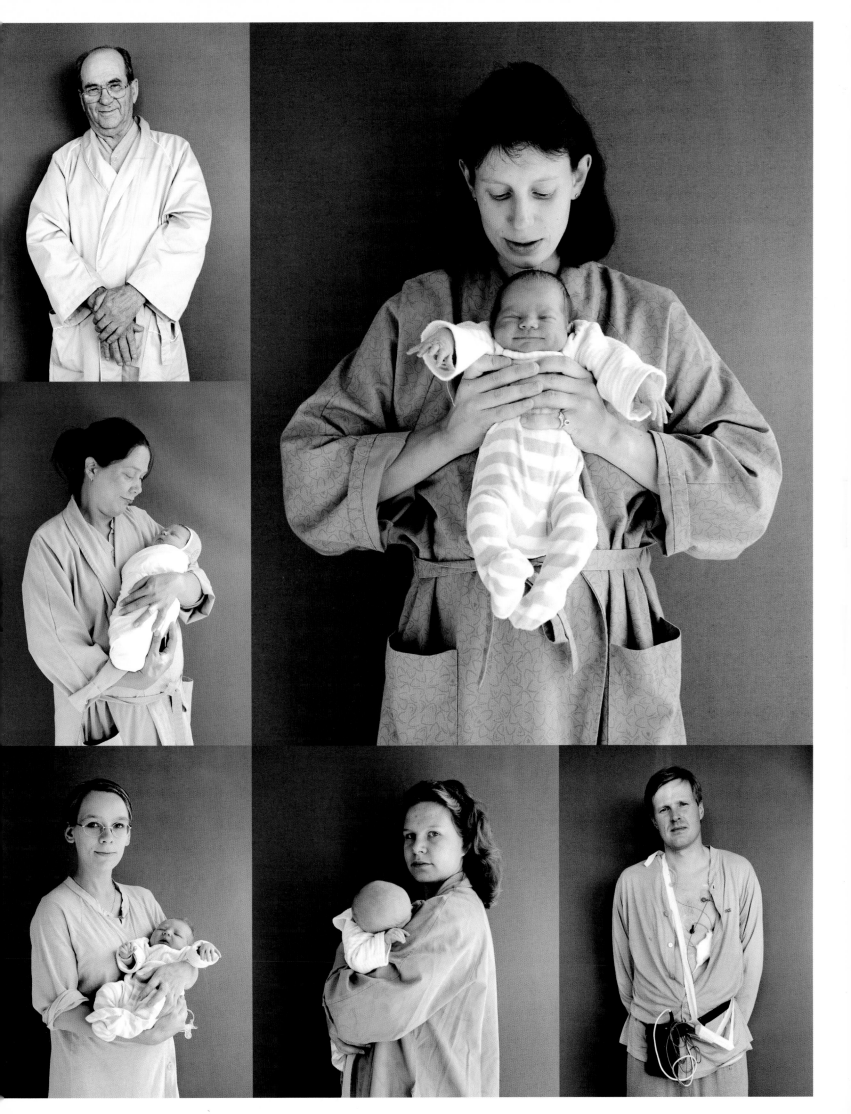

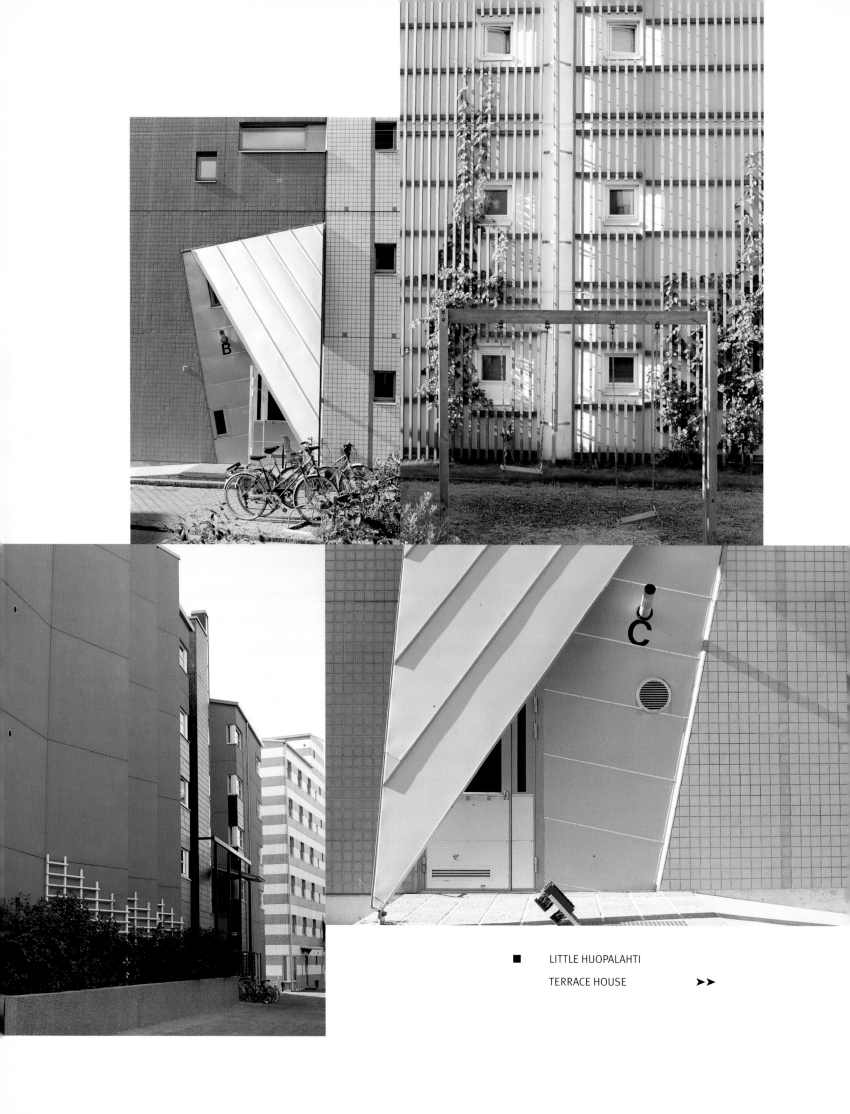

■ LITTLE HUOPALAHTI
TERRACE HOUSE ➤➤

A home at last

Jonni Roos

One raw chilly evening, shopping just before closing time, I saw two odd looking strollers. A young couple were running down Tilkankatu, which is the dullest street in the sharply disparate suburb of Little Huopalahti. The weren't out for an evening stroll. They looked like they'd already run a fair distance, and could no long run much faster than walking speed. The queer thing was that they were running down the middle of the road, which, especially at night, resounds with screeching car tyres as mad drivers belt down its long, straight length.

Although Helsinki's Little Huopalahti was only a few years old then and the residents were a really mixed bunch, you could see they weren't 'locals'. I tried to pass the matter off without raising my eyebrows because urban culture requires you don't show too much interest. This I would have done if I hadn't burst out laughing.

Puffing a bit, the man said to the woman: "Hey, those balconies look rather well looked after." It was, I suppose, a favourable observation.

It was obvious they were a couple of architectural students on a quick visit, rather like the American tourists I saw as a kid at the Olympia Terminal reading a book entitled "Europe in 14 Days".

I bet those students got the popular impression of Little Huopalahti as a nerve-racking and rootless area. Why otherwise run. Having lived there for seven years I can say that Little Huopalahti and the extensive green areas around it form a very balanced totality.

To the delight of my disciplined friend Little Huopalahti is, however, inevitably rather compulsive. Discipline is something completely alien to an area which has sprouted on wasteland like a weed. And for that I'm content. It brings to mind everything that was rough and wild in the old southern districts of Helsinki and that was swept under the carpet during the Eighties.

Little Huopalahti is like Baudelaire's "great whore, who misses little (misses little, but in reality misses everything) in order to look like a fine lady." Making up is a tough job, but Baudelaire was not interested in that. As a resident I am happy to note that psychologists, foreigners and artists (with the exception of architects) have made their home in Little Huopalahti. Oh, and families too. Even the colours of the houses have been adjusted to those of prams.

Discipline is practiced elsewhere, in Ruoholahti for instance. Ruoholahtians would never dream of living in the screaming stimulating carpet "on top of the quaking quagmire" of Little Huopalahti, and neither could Little Huopalahtians imagine living in a "Polish concrete jungle" like Ruoholahti. Two different mentalities are expressed in the urban space: sophisticated and reserved, anarchistic and spontaneous.

Despite being reserved Ruoholahti is progressive: The five-year-old boy dressed in a real fur coat and the lonely man in his worn after-ski boots I saw one winter's eve near the Ruoholahti skating rink, may well live in the same house. The main door of their house is locked like they usually are in the centre and the yard tries to hide behind the gaunt shoulders of the building. The deformed beauty of the surrounding factory and shipyard milieu gives the area a powerful realism and depth in time and activity: Helsinki is more than puckered curtains and rose bushes. The skillfully completed canal breathes life into the whole area.

Also the wastelands, shipyard and oil terminal in East Helsinki have made way for gay and colourful buildings. The forgotten outskirts of

145

the town have been filled with playgrounds, enclosed gardens, new communities meeting in clubs and tenants' associations. The new residents take their dogs for walks and decorate their balconies. And high above all this is the promise of a Home.

The town being built in Vuosaari is the size of Hämeenlinna. The spruce woods that typify the area are being felled to make way for nimble colourful apartment blocks. What a wonderful opportunity was missed when nobody thought how well the spruce forest and the exotic smell of coffee rising from Paulig's roastery suited the urban milieu of Vuosaari, because more people of foreign extraction live there than anywhere else in Helsinki.

■

OLD VUOSAARI

One Marjaniemian had an original idea when he hung from his balcony, opposite the spruce forest, a romantic sign reading Trädgårdsgatan - Garden Way. And what kind of ideal home is needed by that Turkish-looking man with the black moustache, sheepskin coat and wide-brimmed hat striding towards the Carelian Home Bakery in Vuosaari's shopping mall? Does he appreciate the sea view from Vuosaari? The shores are among the most beautiful, but access to the sea is difficult. In many places it is inaccessible to the ordinary residents, especially in Meri-Rastila which was quickly built in the early 1990s on the south point of Vuosaari. Meri-Rastila - Sea Rastila - almost sounds like Venice, but on my first visit there I wandered around for an hour without seeing a glimpse of the sea or anything associated with it. It's quite different on Helsinki's Vironniemi headland which no one thought of calling Meri Ullanlinna.

The buildings extend down to the shore in Vuosaari's new Kallahti, but they look much the same as those in the new part of Herttoniemi which, after all, is quite a different place. They have a lot more in common than the buildings in the new and old parts of Herttoniemi or Vuosaari. This illustrates the great internal migratory movements, one of which is directed at Helsinki, and which caused part of the old spirit of Helsinki to be trampled under foot. I look forward with interest to see what kind of new Helsinki spirit will develop in these areas.

White walls gleaming in their newness may not perhaps give in easily to the man in the sheepskin coat, but more should be done to make them a home. It's difficult to get to grips with these new shining surfaces. Emptiness can really look small and cramped. The smell of plastic flooring tickles the nose and there's still a thin layer of building dust on the corridor floors.

And this I know from my own experience: a bout of frantic furnishing begins. Home! Now! Granny's lamp would look nice on that table. And something to hang on the wall; where's the drill? Mother's busy baking and soon the fridge is full of buns. The television's over there, but where's the antenna cable? There's no need to find a place for the sofa. Familiar objects find safe havens in the white emptiness.

This all makes you feel more settled, although the home is still strange.

Despite all the interior decorating no daring experiments are ventured. Even though the facades of the apartment block have become more multiform, and normally have no wish to disturb the hysterical balance which furnishing a home means. The new buildings of Vuosaari, Herttoniemi, Ruoholahti and Little Huopalahti beckon to their new occupants as though saying: "Welcome! Here is joy and colour. Here it's not gloomy like in a suburb, is it? Is it? It's fun here, isn't it? Isn't it? Please say it's not gloomy here? And one would like to whisper in consent: "No, we don't feel gloomy."

It could be that the woman in the beret with the shoulder bag, now opening her door in the new area of Herttoniemi, has furnished her place in much the same way as the young woman in Vuosaari's Kallahti who took her dog for a walk a moment ago. Do they see a home from their doors? Is it their own home?

Home is a vision of a world that is comprehensible and under control. That's why a home is stranger than truth, but we can't live without it. Each age articulates what makes a home. Time, on the other hand, is full of breaks, gaps, splits, obstacles, but also unexpected bridges. Once the roots have been severed, even a home is closeby. Is it already home? ●

MERI-RASTILA

■ MAY DAY IN KAIVOPUISTO PARK

■   LINNANMÄKI AMUSEMENT PARK

■   MAY DAY

157

■ KORKEASAARI ZOO

Kjäll Westö

It was summer

and I was attending a confirmation class camp on a small island east of Helsinki, almost in the open sea.

At night we'd sneak off behind the rocks to smoke and meet girls from other parishes: in the far west you could see the yellowish glow of the city lighting up the sky. During the day our teacher talked about Hell and damnation, where all pagans and infidels eventually go. I asked him to explain what happened to those people who lived before Christianity was born or who had never heard its message. He thought for a while and said that they would be awakened from the dead and given half-an-hour to make up their minds.

The following morning my pal and I escaped on the Helsinki-bound ferry. It docked at the market square, where we got off. The place smelled of fish and coffee, sea gulls screeched overhead, the more daring ones dive bombing us. We walked through the market, up Esplanade to Stockmann's department store.

>>

On the corner of Keskuskatu and North Esplanade, where the new Stockmann wing is now, there used to be a low wooden building in those days, rather like a barracks, which had a candy stall and smelly hot dog stand. We bought a packet of Kent cigarettes (both our mothers smoked Kent so it was the only brand we knew), sat down on a bench, lit up, and puffing quietly away, gazed at the tall, gaunt buildings around us and the empty early-morning streets. To Hell with damnation! Life and the city were there in front of us, fragrant, smelly, breathing, labyrinthine, full of adventure and mystery.

I was thirteen years old, brought up in a suburban housing estate. I believe it was that morning when I took this town, this awkward and remote northern village as it's often called, to be my very own.

Spring comes to Helsinki hesitantly, dithering like a fairy godmother who can't make up her mind whether she's for good or evil. Every year it misleads migrating birds, first it lures them here by melting the snow and drying the earth, then it pours snow and ice on them once they've arrived. Every year Helsinkians leave off their winter coats too early, don their leather jackets, spring suits or tattered trainers - and then get caught in an April snow storm.

It is night when I write these words. The 27th day of March in the year of grace 1997. Spring has already come to Portugal, it is tassel-time in the trees of Turin, and soon it will be sringtide in Paris. Here it is still winter, storm winds rattle the tin roofs of apartment blocks and there are ice flows on the open sea at Kruunuvuorenselkä. When I nip out onto the balcony for a smoke, the light from the Suomenlinna beacon glimmers faintly through the blizzard, and my leather jacket hangs despondent and unused in the hallway.

But the spring will come. And then I have something the Portuguese and Turinians haven't: I have Helsinki in springlight. This light is the reason why I don't like becoming middle-aged, old. I know what it's like to walk when very young and head-over-heels in love through Helsinki's parks in late May and early June, when the grass smells sweet and the trees are budding. Then the fairy godmother no longer dithers, then she is for good. And in her spell a fire burns within the townsfolk, rising from their hearts to their eyes.

Helsinki, at least the old Helsinki in which I grew up, is a shy city. You can see it in the eyes of the older generation. It's true they attend the festivities, festivals and mega events organised by the city. But they always stand a bit to the side, they smile, their faces have a slightly dubious expression as though saying: "Okay enjoy yourselves now, but tomorrow's it's back to work. And they promise rain." The younger generation, on the other hand, are frightfully continental and have even managed to bring about some changes. The ruthless Lex Helsinki of the growth years of the Seventies no longer rules: anything goes that's not specifically forbidden by law. In recent years the city centre has become more tolerant, more open, especially in summertime. At the same time it has become more expensive, and perhaps even more dangerous

In Helsinki, as in all cities, the youth who live in the suburbs appear to spend their days hanging-out in the centre, whereas the older people seldom go there.

In the early 1980s I lived in the suburb of Kontula, which then had one of the worst reputations in Helsinki. It was quite alright living there, even though the journey downtown was too long, much too long.

Kontula was then very national. In the shopping centre or on the late night buses you heard Finnish and only Finnish spoken.

The other autumn I visited Kontula after an absence of more than ten years. My son had a football match there.

Gangs of youth hung around the field, just like in the old days. But now the lads in one gang spoke Somali, and those in another Russian.

On the threshold of the new millennium, Helsinki is changing, both the suburbs and the centre. Soon it may be as international as it was at the beginning of the century, but in a different way, naturally.

In what way?

Well, that's something the city doesn't know yet.

When you have lived in a town for long enough, it becomes transformed into a series of memories; I worked in that building for so-and-so, I used to visit that café for a coffee and cinnamon bun after I'd taken my kid to the kindergarten, the girl with the brown eyes and shy smile lived in that house, in that one I wrote a book and listened to the tempting jingle of the ice-cream man at five in the afternoon, in that street was the restaurant where I once had too much to drink and ...

Helsinki is a city where - with good luck that is - you can land yourself a shimmering silver fish very close to the centre, off the shores of the islands of Suomenlinna, Pihlajasaari or Lauttasaari. I've sometimes had this dream where I take the ferry to Suomenlinna and catch me a beautiful trout. I carefully remove the hook from it's jaws, lift it high up so it can see the city and say: "There's the water where I swim. It's not so beautiful or even so free as in your world, but then I'm only a pale-faced street ant, not a wild and silvery missile like you."

Then I let the fish go and take the ferry back to town. ●

VALLILA SUMMER CHALET SETTLEMENT

Midsummer enlightenments

Summer, flies and cold beer. And whatever you say, you can't beat Midsummer: Christmas may be the finest, but a Midsummer dance is worth going through Hell for. If anyone dares to

■ VATTUNIEMI

doubt that Midsummer in Helsinki is not worth its weight in gold, then they can't ever have been on the Island. And neither have they such genuine mates as Arvi happens to have: perhaps Teukka and Ratilainen have never swum in a lake, but even to them the sea gives the real background to Midsummer. Just as it does to the darts board on the wall of Ratilainen's little red cabin.

"Mr Toivonen, this is the last one," says the bloke in overalls with exaggerated ceremony and Toivonen looks really pleased inspecting his brand-new ice hockey goal. In the nearby warehouse there are a dozen more, just under the sights of a 1:2 scale-model Mustang fighter.

What is it? Blade runner for some future Helsinki? A beached Noah's Ark from the past? Santa Claus' workshop in some other reality? No, just Mr Toivonen's ark here and now, creator of droll creatures to populate Helsinki's parks.

"I remember the day the slump began, it was autumn," says Toivonen, ex-landscape gardener, and goes to talk about the Japanese garden in the woods of Roihuvuori. Apart from wooden sculptures and special gardens, his programme also includes flowering meadows. Even a disused 60-hectare rubbish tip is being returned to nature.

For more than five years, tools in hand, over 400 unemployed have toiled on half-year employment schemes. A fair number of ordinary animal kingdoms have been created, also a few ships and lighthouses, a mobile greenhouse and the world's largest miniature hockey game (about 2.7 m x 4.5 m), says Toivonen listing what they've done. "When people want something amusing, they turn to us."

And the place, in Toivonen's opinion, is the best possible: army manoeuvres ensure its guarded free of charge. Of course, the

Rescue Service comes and burns the odd car, but it also puts them out again. All other costs have to be covered from selling the products: rent, furniture, machines, your own and the boss's wages. So it's no miracle if entirely new species are created occasionally, like this fish-fowl: the top half looks like an eel and the under part resembles a pig. "What d'you think of it?" asks Toivonen without expecting a reply.

But even quite ordinary species have been created here, like the Savonlinna rubber tree, for instance. Once someone had thought up the idea of mixing bits of rubber, plywood and plastic together, adding wax to form blocks, and finally a bit of Savonlinna business acumen, our recycled flora gained a rubber tree. "We've even got a representative abroad, in Turkey," grins the rubber tree merchant, who, living up to his name (which means a little hope), dwells in the nether land between hope and faith. ●

In the crackle of urban warfare, a new life takes form in East

Toivonen's Ark

Helsinki. A fish-fowl has just acquired terrestrial shape and within the great concrete hall lies Noah's Ark in two pieces – its passengers waiting patiently, standing around in idle

Harri Ruohomäki

disparate groups outside and partly inside too: over there are horses and foals, further away a drove of juicy hares, across the yard are black terriers ears alert and a flock of puffins loaf in the sauna-stove heated warehouse. And then this fish-fowl thing.

Midsummer! Mad-summer! Taking the sweet, honeyed steam in probably the only sauna on the Island, then a cool dip in the sea and, even though the accusing finger of industrial society points directly at the barbecue charcoal bag left by the gentlemen on the shore, a Finn - especially a Helsinkian - would never be at a loss when faced with the ritual task of grilling sausages.

But not even three guys can get a Midsummer dance going, even if - how shall I put it - this well lubricated stomping trio tries its best to improvise on the rocky shore. To the point of passing out. Particularly Teukka's and Ratilainen's passing out, as Arvi's wandering in the hereafter and back during the nightless night has just begun.

Whether it was due to his desire for a dancing partner or what, Arvi had decided to take a certain distance from the matter at hand and pushed off in his own element from the shore in Ratilainen's boat. It was good fun rowing the little boat by yourself but there was no reason to overdo it. After a while even Arvi had decided to give in to the joys of Midsummer and stretched out in the bottom of the boat in the warmth of the morning sun. His mind was so serene watching the clouds sail by and contemplating the world in general.

In the soft rocking of the sea Arvi thus forgot all his earthly worries and his eyes closed with the gentle even rolling. If Arvi noticed anything in his innocent dreaming, he would have realised that the waves were carrying him to new waters, distant shores. Actually right to the other end of the Island - as seen from Ratilainen's hut.

The bow of the boat bumped against the sandy shore, the rocking movement somehow changed its nature and Arvi opened his eyes. And he was convinced that he had entered the Pearly Gates in reward for his modest good deeds. So indescribably innocent and wonderful were the faces of the angels that looked down upon him from the brightness above. Firm but friendly angelic hands helped Arvi from his earthly vehicle, if a boat could be called such in the heavenly atmosphere surrounding him: accompanied by the sweet songs of birds Arvi stepped onto the soft sand, the warm sea caressing his slightly numbed feet.

And what can a man of the world do in a situation like this: fall down on his knees naturally and try to express his gratitude to these angelic figures - even kiss the slender pale feet in front of him. First the feet of one heavenly messenger and then another, but soon another and perhaps even one more. Arvi's feeling was sincere and genuine, this you could see from his submissiveness.

It could be that Arvi's gratitude was partly due to the about knee high legs of one of the angels when it happened. A tremendous bang as though the heavens had burst asunder! At first nothing else was heard or felt, but in a moment Arvi's backside that was humbly pointed upwards almost burst into flames. And a split second latter another explosion. This time the flames came quicker and Arvi, on his knees in the sand, rolled over to somehow control the situation.

The sun was blotted out by this colossal giant on whose shoulders, according to Arvi's account, rose thick clusters of long hair to the heavens. Good and evil! Good and evil are struggling for my soul was Arvi's lightening explanation of the situation and he started to draw conclusions. And soon it was time for analyses, as the equivalent of that Beelzebub had again lifted the oar borrowed from Ratilainen's boat and would this time have caused flames more likely on the other side of Arvi's backside.

And how it yelled! Even when Arvi had thrown himself into the bottom of Ratilainen's boat, a thunderous noise was heard from the direction of the shore. Lying on his stomach in the boat Arvi paddled with his hands and, once the worst had died down, carefully rose to sit at the stern and began rowing with the sole remaining oar toward more familiar shores. But Arvi never looked back, for in his imagination good always triumphed over evil.

●

Harri Ruohomäki

■ VARSASAARI IS A HOLIDAY
PARADISE FOR HELSINKIANS,
ONLY 5 MINUTES AWAY BY BOAT.

What are little sportsmen made of?

Liisa looked at her children who had fallen asleep from exhaustion after the evening's training, and thought of the old nursery rhyme: What are little boys made of, What are little girls ... Well, they're still made of pretty different things, whether you like it or not, that a mother has to admit.

The puny little, hockey-playing lad is dressed in a uniform so as to look like a man. Put his armour on, just like a knight, the main thing is to look bigger than he is. The lively and strapping little girl, on the other hand, has clothes removed to reveal all the contours of her body. The girl learns to look as small as possible.

■ HELSINKI OLYMPIC STADIUM

The boy is taught to fight against others, to meet his opponent eye to eye, to clash in the sweet smell of battle. The girl is taught to move harmoniously in line, to avoid colliding and competing.

For the boy being selected for the team is an important decision. In Helsinki hockey players are members of either HIFK or Jokerit. At matches the fathers compete in yelling support for their sons, from the stands. The men's matches always demand a momumental arena, a suitable background for heroes.

The girl exercises in school gyms or club rooms, and no particular status is attached to the association's name. The special tour de force, however, was the Women's Gymnastic Association's centenary in 1996. Some 30 000 women from all over Finland gathered at the Helsinki Olympic Stadium to perform together. In some families there were as many as four generations housed at the schools and performing on the field - women's gymnastics is a life-long activity, you never need to transfer to the stands.

During the last hundred years, however, something has fundamentally changed. Boys and girls are no longer brought up in such rigidly different castes. Under her flying skirts my daughter has trimmed muscles. And when she removes her frilly performance costume, she prefers to dress in a T-shirt, shorts and trainers - just like her brother. She enjoys competing, and these days it's allowed. Only in the last couple of years have competitions been held in traditional Finnish women's gymnastics; before then the idea was frowned upon.

More and more girls want to play ice hockey, preferably ferociously, rather than a softer game like ringette. On the other hand, women's gymnastic associations have taken on boys seeking something else than the blood, sweat and tears of traditional sports.

Hip hop and street dance draw more young men than it's possible to take on. In aerobics even the lads acquire a colourful appearance and flirt with the audience. Even they, apparently, like being the centre of attraction.

Something is also happening to the smaller ice-hockey boys. You can see pony tails peeking out from under their helmets, tied with a fashionable band, and rings glissen in their ears. The little man's uniform is not so uniform any more.

Moreover, ice-hockey heroes are setting a new style for men: when he was younger, the Finnish NHL hockey player Teemu Selänne worked in a daycare centre. Now the father of a small son, he still works for the benefit of children. These changes are only problematic for middle-aged men. Liisa wonders how to get Pentti interested in something else than ringside sports, to move other than by car, and to sweat at something else than just watching his own son's matches. A forlorn hope it seems, even though many less sportive men go walking and do back exercises.

Walking alongside her loveable lump Liisa has to smile a bit: Pentti's bulging belly seems so reassuring. After all, little girls and little boys grow up to a different kind of life. ●

Anna-Stiina Nykänen

175

HELSINKI CUP

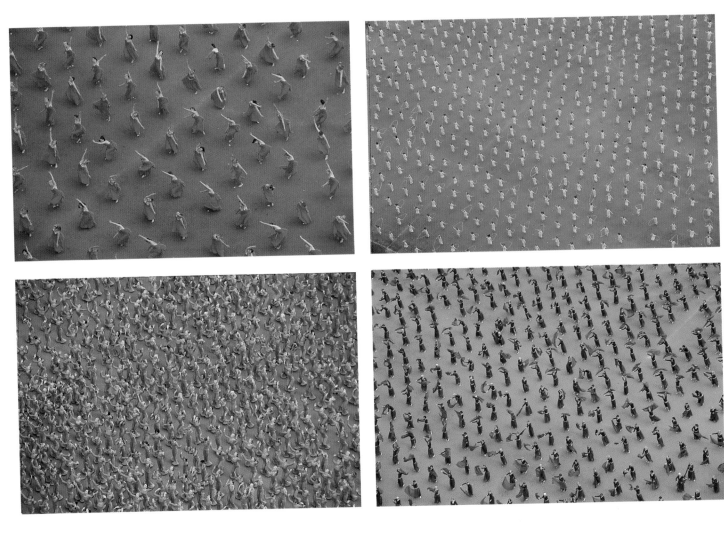

CENTENARY CELEBRATIONS OF
WOMEN'S GYMNASTICS AT THE
OLYMPIC STADIUM

Malmi

The people of Malmi work in modern offices and chop wood for the sauna under the shade of lilac trees. There are families where as many as three generations have attended the same schools and whose former teachers are well remembered in the area. Nowadays, these schools are part of Helsinki's huge educational system. At some of them not even one out of ten of the teachers lives in Malmi. Private shopkeepers stubbornly survive alongside the supermarkets and ever encroaching chainstores. New times may crush the homely corner foodstores, but not the florists, goldsmiths and watchmakers, small dress stores, photographers, Malmi born-and-bred cobblers, or the bookshop dating from the 1920s. Such entrepreneurs still have the knack and take time to chat with their customers whilst wrapping their purchases. In the super stores few shoppers say anything to the friendly check-out girls. A school from the 1920s and Kristian Gullichsen's church from 1981 face each other across the four-lane road - the centuries old highway to Häme.   >

Aarne Laurila

Next to the school is the youth association's building from 1913. It is Swedish-speaking, like the majority of Malmians from the middle ages to quite recently; even after the second world war both of the local health officers were Swedish-speaking. At the beginning of this century workers began moving from Helsinki and the countryside to live alongside the Malmi railway. These hundreds became thousands. Industrial Malmi, which existed until the 1960s, produced Finland's first car bodies, it made pots, canned fish, lemonade, ovens, zip fasteners, bricks, swatches, roofing felt, nails, metal fittings and many types of agricultural machines. Bread and Easter **mämmi** were made by Tikkala's Mama, the mother of singer Arvi Tikkala, and sold in Helsinki's market square. During the second world war grenade casings and chips for wood-gas generators were produced.

The Civil War was hard on Red Malmi - one of the victims being the local cooperative society - but between the wars Malmi became the centre of Helsinki Rural District, rather like a parish without a church. The hospital opened in 1908 gradually expanded and diversified. Malmi Airport became operative in 1936. The Malmi cemetery, established by the parishes of Helsinki in the 1890s, eventually became the largest in the country. The embankment of the cemetery railway line - conveying both the living and the dead - is now an asphalted pathway down which expensive-looking dogs are walked and little boys rollerblade at high speed. Of the past many Helsinkians recall the legendary Malmi Romanies. In recent times Malmi became a refugee centre, something which suits a place where diversity is a tradition. During the war the airport was run by the Germans, and afterwards by the Soviets under the Allied Control Commission.

The development of Malmi as a peripheral town ceased with the district mergers of 1946. Helsinki Rural District - which eventually became the borough and then the town of Vantaa - moved its administration to Tikkurila. Factories began to close down and the huge decorative villas fell into disrepair and were gradually demolished. One of them was the villa where the young Axel Gallén lived in the 1890s and painted his famous Aino triptych. Helsinki invested in new suburbs until it realised the potential of these old villages.

In 1972 the decision was taken to transform Malmi into the area centre for northeast Helsinki. By the mid-1990s it had over 12 000 inhabitants - about 85 000 altogether in the northeastern area - and 6 000 jobs. In the 1980s a new railway station was built, as well as a vast complex of shops, restaurants, banks, offices and a swimming baths. In 1994 the Malmi House cultural and educational centre was opened. The 1920s' wooden youth building on the corner of an urban concrete square looks like something from a Wild West town and indeed the builder had actually been in America. The statue erected by the city in the square reminds locals of a gigantic MacDonald's M and is slowly rusting away: didn't the bigwigs know that iron rusts? At the annual Old Malmi dance you waltz to the music of the Malmi Lads whose average age is about seventy and even Florida is conquered - in the hall of the School for Social Welfare Studies. During the day students learn how to care for the young and the old, for the socially excluded and the unemployed. Even in Malmi there are all types. Like the rest of Helsinki, many holiday abroad, go to summer houses or ski centres; others study foreign trade in English at the commercial college. In the verdant surroundings pheasants peck in the gardens and hares frolic in the early evening dusk. And hedgehogs are fed from spring to autumn. ●

193

Ice cream winter

It was a cold evening, but it's always like that at first.
Jani grimaced thinking that soon it will be nice and
warm in the cab and nice and cool in the back.
It's never the same.

"I heard they even killed one driver in Sweden, but even so I still think it's worthwhile doing this."

A cold job for cool men in the wild north.

"There's this doggie that comes with a bag in its mouth. The lolly and order are in the bag, I just put in what it says. At Länsimäki this big bloke comes for his order with his dog. Business is thriving."

"This is a service profession," Jani stressed to himself, "And every evening it's a matter of life and death: if you're five minutes late then even grown-ups throw potatoes at you from the balcony. If you play the jingle then some bloke comes and threatens to fetch his shot gun and blast you if he hears another sound, for Christ's sake."

Jani had to start the van up on slippery snow - it's been snowing again - and behind him there's another one trying to straighten up first, but only manages to get even closer. Rally drivers!

"One bloke cut the wires with pliers on my mate's cab because he couldn't stop the jingle in time."

There's money in Helsinki. People buying and selling, its always been like that. And when one sells the daily groceries, it adds a little extra to somebody else's life. They say that the markets are developing, expanding and deepening. **"This is one of those forms of cooperation, not so very official like, but there's nout wrong with it either to my mind. It's a bit like being in the same boat together, which is what we are."** *"I don't know the guy from Adam, but once he gave me a plastic bag full of sprats when the fishmonger behind me was doing so well."* | Helsinki's such a big city that there are even people in it who don't always remember to pay for their shopping. I'm not mentioning any particular district, like, even people move.

Dusk descends quickly over Helsinki, the day's not very long at this latitude at this time of the year. I bring a message of joy to homes and offices every evening. The round varies, as the customers are never cast in the same mould. Apart from the regulars, that is.

Harri Ruohomäki

197

At the beginning of 1997 there were 532 800 people living in Helsinki. As the annual increase is estimated at 4 400, by 2000 the population will be 547 000 and by 2015 about 575 000.

Aarne Laurila

Compared to the postwar period, the city is ever more interested in highly-educated youth. Nationwide migration to the larger connurbations has brought people to the greater metropolitan area. Helsinki considers the capital's dynamicism beneficial, if not indispensable, to the whole nation.

In the 1990s the role of cities in international competition has grown, whereas that of nations has relatively declined. Helsinki emphasises its reliable services: municipal utilities and public transport function well - the water and waters are clean - the city is safe. Advanced technology is available. Through its efforts in developing cultural and business activities in the city centre, Helsinki expresses its confidence in the urban life style. Helsinki has its own representatives in Brussels, at the hub of the EU. Both Helsinki and Moscow have centres in each others city centres providing information and marketing assistance, building contacts and renting space for companies. There is also systematic cooperation with St. Petersburg and Tallinn.

Helsinki invests in education - both the city and its inhabitants are aware of the danger that the sharp division between the employed and the unemployed, between those with a command or ignorance of information technology and foreign languages, will differentiate people from each other. To ensure the continuous availability of knowledge, schools and libraries have been provided with information technology equipment and the Finnish and Swedish Adult Education Centres with a diversity of courses. Training in art and communications has been radically increased.

Helsinki admits that the future is uncertain, but is confident that the importance of the environment will increase. The cleanliness, beauty and richness of the environment are important values both to the city's inhabitants and to international activities from tourism to investment. Helsinkians have continuously expressed their concern with the future of the environment in respect to two major projects, the Viikki Science Park and residential estate, and the great new harbour at Vuosaari. Will building at Viikki threaten the Old Town bay nature conservation area and its unique habitats? What effect will the harbour have on the waters, landscape and nature in general? The city authorities have justified the harbour not only on economic

grounds, but also environmentally: as the city's waterfront is freed for housing, this will reduce heavy-duty traffic in the centre and increase transportation by sea. The phased construction of the Viikki Science Park on the lands of an historic manor, and which will provide some six thousand jobs in research and production, is based on a thorough understanding of surrounding nature. Ecological questions have played a conspicuous role in the research work the city has conducted or commissioned. Specific areas of study have included the consumption and management of energy, heat and water, and the erection of wooden apartment blocks. The objectives behind making Töölö Bay fit for swimmers are ecological and aesthetic, those behind improving element building are aesthetic and economic. More beautiful concrete facades are awarded prizes. Through high-density building the town spares the environment and through supporting a public transport system, particularly rail transport, it reduces the environmental hazards of traffic.

The rights and needs of nature and people? Speed and fertile quietude, activity and good-natured indolence? The appreciation of the different ages of Helsinki and new building that will not impair its spiritual aspect? These are the questions asked from all, from the decision-maker in his office or in the field, from each Helsinkian individually, each in his own way. ●

On the rim of Helsinki

■ ONLY IN ONE PLACE DOES HELSINKI EXTEND BEYOND THE RING III, MOTORWAY, ITS SYMBOLIC BORDER

THE HELSINKI BOOK AND CD-ROM HAVE BEEN PRODUCED BY
THE CITY OF HELSINKI IN COOPERATION WITH THE UNIVERSITY
OF ART AND DESIGN'S DEPARTMENT OF PHOTOGRAPHY.

Commissioned by: The City of Helsinki, Special
          Publications Committee
Chairman: Aarne Laurila
Members: Juha Föhr, Irina Krohn, Pekka Saarnio *and*
          Lauri Törhönen

Pertti Mustonen, The City of Helsinki, Information Office
Kristina Niklander *and* Tarja Raivio

Students from the University of Art and Design's Department of
Photography took the pictures for the Helsinki Book during the
academic year 1995-1996.

Photographers:
    Nanni Akkola 19, 24, 25, 27, 55, 62,79
    Nils Andersson 181
    Satu Autero 20-23
    Taru Blomstedt 25, 34-35, 37, 67, 98-99
    Elina Brotherus 50, 114, 197
    Taneli Eskola 176, 186-190
    Ulla Hassinen 94-97, 121, 123
    Maarit Hohteri 113
    Hanna Hämäläinen 152, 158, 167-169
    Vuokko Isoherranen 56
    Sanna Kannisto 141-143
    Sandra Kantanen 28-29
    Ari Karttunen 84, 144-145
    Jaana Laakko 112-113, 152, 173
    Andrej Lajunen 102-107
    Heini Lehväslaiho 87-92, 125
    Laura Malmivaara 184-185
    Johanna Mannila 174, 181
    Leena Markkanen 39, 58, 62, 78
    Mikko Mälkki 32-33 (*work group*), 60-61 (*work group*),
        70-71, 80 (*work group*), 134-135 (*work group*),
        200-202
    Seppo Niiranen 13-17, 63-68, 73-75
    Pekka Nikrus 51-53, 110-111, 116-117, 146-147
        (*work group*), 150-151,153-156, 161-164, 174,
        177-180, 182-183
    Elina Orpana 94-97
    Selja Palmu 76
    Patrik Pesonius 123
    Marja Pursiainen 42-45, 77, 85
    Sirpa Päivinen 35, 54, 72, 114-115, 160, 165, 168-169
    Riitta Päiväläinen 57, 148-149, 172, 173
    Merja Salo 150
    Mika Seppälä 72
    Anu Suhonen 86, 93, 112-113, 120, 181
    Heidi Söderholm 72
    Elina Söyri 127-131
    Ilkka Tolonen 158, 170-172, 184, 194-197
    Tommi Tuomi 122
    Juha Törmälä 30-31, 36, 38 (*work group*), 47-49, 55, 69,
        75, 80, 82-83, 100-101 (*work group*), 108-109
        (*work group*), 118-119, 124-125, 132-133 (*work
        group*), 192-193 (*work group*)
    Tuukka Uusitalo 125
    Eeva Vierros 137-138

Director of Photography: Merja Salo
Text editor: Harri Ruohomäki
Digital processing of photographs: Pekka Nikrus

Authors:
   Aarne Laurila, *PhD.*
   Riitta Nikula, *professor*
   Anna-Stiina Nykänen, *journalist*
   Antti Raivio, *theatre director*
   Jonni Roos, *arts journalist*
   Harri Ruohomäki, *media consultant*
   Pirkko Saisio, *professor and author*
   Märta Tikkanen, *writer*
   Kjell Westö, *writer*

Graphic design and layout: Tapio Vapaasalo *and* Pekka Nikrus

Translation: Michael Wynne-Ellis

Printers: F.G. Lönnberg, Helsinki, 1998

ISBN 951-718-126-4

The following persons were responsible for the enclosed CD-ROM:

Photographers:
   Satu Autero: A short history of Helsinki
   Taru Blomstedt and Harri Laakso: Intersections
   Elina Brotherus: Portrait of an artist
   Ulla Hassinen *and* Elina Orpana: Shopping small is beautiful
   Waleska Heeb: Ice hockey!
   Christian Jakowleff: The Helsinki underground
   Sanna Kannisto: From sickness to health
   Väinö Kannisto: The war (*compiled by* Merja Salo, Jari Harju,
      Riitta Pakarinen *and* Sari Koskinen)
   Andrei Lajunen: From the blue
   Seppo Niiranen: View of 360°
   Pekka Nikrus: Helsinki Cup
   Pekka Nikrus: Off-season
   Riitta Päiväläinen: At home
   Riitta Päiväläinen: At the market place
   Mika Seppälä *and* Heidi Söderholm: Corner encounters
   Elina Söyri: The multicultural city
   Iikka Tolonen: Cruisin' night
   Iikka Tolonen, Andrei Lajunen, Jaana Laakko: Ice cream winter
   Juha Törmälä *and* Nanni Akkola: The purity of neo-classicism
   Juha Törmälä, Mikko Mälkki, Pekka Nikrus, Nanni Akkola
      and Ari Karttunen: What's a true Helsinkian like?
   Eeva Vierros: Small families

Director of the CD-ROM production group: Seppo Niiranen
Compilation and programming: Seppo Niiranen, Pekka Nikrus, Taru
      Blomstedt, Harri Laakso, Eija Hiltunen, Suvi Sillanpää, Sari Koskinen
Programming consultant: Hannu Riihimäki
CD-ROM design: Seppo Niiranen
Text editor: Harri Ruohomäki
Texts: Märta Tikkanen, Harri Ruohomäki, Seppo Niiranen *and* City of Helsinki,
      Information Management Center
Translation: Valtasana Oy/Tytti Laine, Raija Jänicke, Michael Wynne-Ellis

Musical composition and technical realisation: Antti Ikonen
Musicians: Antti Ikonen (keyboard), Berislav Jurisic (winds),
      Juha Levo (bass), Johanna Lögren (accordion),
      Nora Rissanen (violin)
Sound post production: Ari Outila
Special sound effects: Jaska Uimonen, Juha Torvinen, Uljas Pulkkis
Narrations: Maria Salo, Tauno Pajukallio, Glyn Banks, Mira Berglund
Post production of narrations: Geert Braam

Acknowledgemets: Medialab/UIAH: Philip Dean, Hannu Riihimäki, Lily Diaz,
      Lauri Mäkelä; Mediabrewery/HUT, Pia Sivenius (Dept. of
      Photography/UIAH), Esa Katajamäki (City of Helsinki Information
      Management Centre)